ATLANTIS:
AS BELOW SO ABOVE
A SPIRITUAL ODYSSEY

ATLANTIS:
AS BELOW SO ABOVE

A SPIRITUAL ODYSSEY

**Lindsey Elizabeth Day
and
Spiritual Artist, Marion Lawrence**

Copyright © Lindsey Elizabeth Day 2021

All rights reserved. No part of this publication may be reproduced or transmitted in any form or by any means, electronic or mechanical including photocopying, recording or any information storage or retrieval system, without prior permission in writing from the publishers.

The right of Lindsey Elizabeth Day to be identified as the author of this work has been asserted by her in accordance with the Copyright, Designs and Patent Act 1988.

First published in the United Kingdom in 2021 by

The Cloister House Press

ISBN 978-1-913460-41-9

The image on the Front Cover of
**ATLANTIS: AS BELOW SO ABOVE
A SPIRITUAL ODYSSEY**
is a copy of an encaustic painting
by Marion Lawrence.
She called it,
A Leap of Faith.

**This book is dedicated to
The Great Soul of Light Supreme**

Also By The Author

The Cherishing

The Diviner Mysteries:
A Course on Mystical Revelation

The Meditative Thread:
A Prophetic Poem of Peace

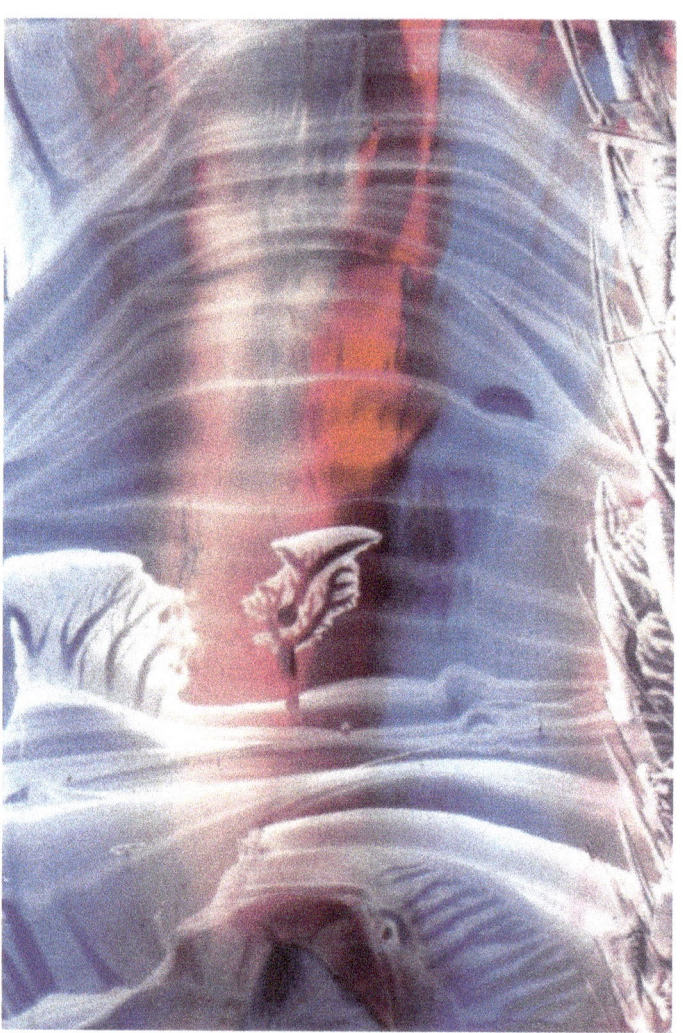

CONTENTS

Dedication — 5

Acknowledgements
- A Leap of Faith — 12

Foreword
- The Kingdom of Heaven — 15

The Atlantean Mystery & The Great Event
- Be Still and Know — 19

The Acolyte
- Crystal Cities of Atlantis — 27

The Scribe
- Part I – The Novice
- The Sphinx — 41
- Part II – The Initiate
- Journey Through the Labyrinth — 63

The Witness
- Part I – The Alliance
- Gateway to Atlantis — 81
- Part II – The Special Message
- The Dark Clouds — 99

The Messenger
- Transformation — 111

Meditation
- Take the Path   129

The Higher Self
- Heaven is on Earth   137

As Above, So Below
- Universal Wisdom   141

Thanksgiving
- I Am Always Here   145

Recommended Reading
- Tibetan Buddhist Prayer   149

Contact
- Magic   153

Afterword
- Grace of The Way   157

(Illustrations on Pages 31, 36, 46, 54-59 and 65 are by the Author)

ACKNOWLEDGEMENTS

A LEAP OF FAITH

*Take a chance.
When you take the first step,
the Angels will help you.*

MARION LAWRENCE

I am very grateful to Loni Armstrong for giving me a box of Marion Lawrence's Spirit Art Cards for my birthday as they are a marvellous aid to meditation.

In addition, I want to say a great big thank you to Marion for her kindness in letting me include some of her cards from the box, as well as other cards that she has given me, in **ATLANTIS: AS BELOW SO ABOVE, A SPIRITUAL ODYSSEY**. The card on the front cover, which is entitled, *A Leap of Faith,* is relevant to the content of the whole of this book.

Marion calls the encaustic paintings *Inner Landscapes of the Soul*. They were channelled by her, along with the messages, while deep in meditation and they incorporate ancient knowledge and wisdom.

My dear friend, Jane Miles' unflagging interest in the progress that I was making whilst I was writing this book meant a great deal to me. Bless you, Jane.

FOREWORD

THE KINGDOM OF HEAVEN

*The Angels keep their ancient places;
Turn but a stone, and start a wing!
'Tis ye, 'tis your estranged faces,
That miss the many-splendoured thing.*[1]

FRANCIS THOMPSON

When the Atlantean Age was at its peak, to the Ancient Egyptians it would have seemed as though Atlantis was Heaven on Earth and the powers possessed by the Atlanteans, would have made the Egyptians believe that the Atlanteans were Gods and Goddesses.

Those who came from the Atlantean Race certainly have missed the 'many splendoured' lifestyle that they once knew. Although there have been numerous attempts, through the ages, to establish a Society that lived up to the time of the Atlantean idyll, they have all failed. Why was this so? Will it ever be possible for the 'Kingdom of Heaven' to be on Earth again and if it is, where will it be located?

I will be answering these questions after I have shared with you a little of my history concerning the Atlantean Mystery but first of all, I am going to ask *you* a question as it is relevant to what will ensue.

---

[1] Selected Poems, Francis Thompson

THE ATLANTEAN MYSTERY AND THE GREAT EVENT

BE STILL AND KNOW

Be still, and know that
when you are in the
Spiritual Realms of the Angels,
you are guided and protected.

MARION LAWRENCE

Have you wondered why you are on Earth at this particular time? It is because of the special knowledge that you gained during one or more of your previous lifetimes. Unless regression is undergone, or the intention is set before meditating to access one or more of your past lives, they are not usually remembered. As a result, you may not realise the noteworthy contribution that you are making by appearing in the 'film' that is being shown on Earth at present. It is called, *The Great Event,* and it is a remake.

The original 'film' called, *The Great Event,* was made a very long time ago, but it is still remembered. It could be that it has remained in our consciousness as a warning. In other words, this is what can happen to a civilisation if it tries to harness forces that are far more powerful than can be understood in human terms, and then does not abide by the cosmic laws that govern those forces.

Before the destruction of Atlantis, there was a general decline in the spiritual growth that had been attained when the Atlantean Age was at its peak. Particular attention needs to be paid to this as a high degree of spiritual development is crucial when the rate at which technological advances escalates otherwise a Fall, or something even worse, can easily occur. If things go so wrong that there is a danger that a civilisation could cause the destruction of Earth, the whole of the 'film' may be wiped and everything will have to begin again.

This will not happen to our Civilisation. The remake will have a different ending. A revolution of spiritual consciousness will take place and the level of spiritual advancement that will occur will ensure that our Civilisation will be operating from a base that is very much more secure than it was before. It is vital that you do not give up your faith that Atlantis will re-emerge. Its importance must never be underestimated. "Faith is the substance of things hoped for"[1] and evidence that these things are going to manifest can be obtained during meditation. It is an excellent way to renew your faith, for there is a vast amount of knowledge stored below the waves of consciousness that can be accessed while 'in the Spirit.' Indeed, the Atlantean Mystery can only be clarified, and the true reality realised, whilst in a deep state of meditation.

I was taught how to meditate at the Maharishi Mahesh Yogi School of Transcendental Meditation, in Kent, over 25 years ago. The spiritual experiences that I will be describing and all the information that is in **ATLANTIS: AS BELOW SO ABOVE, A SPIRITUAL ODYSSEY** has been attained purely through meditation techniques alone as I have never used hallucinogenic drugs of any kind.

[1] Hebrews 11:1

In the meditation that is near the end of this book, I have set out one of the ways that I enter into the meditative state. Meditation is like a revolving door through which you can gain entry to the Inner World and then, whenever you wish to do so, you can go back through the door and out into the Material World again. As a result, there is no need to be anxious about visiting the Higher Realms of the Inner World.

When you take a Leap of Faith and venture into those Realms, apart from meeting Angels and/or Archangels; Ascended and Higher Ascended Masters, and enlightened ones with whom you had a connection with in one or more of your past lives, all manner of Advanced Beings will come forward once you have set the intention, of the meditation, to find out more knowledge about Atlantis. They will help you with your quest and so that you can gain understanding of the subtleties *(the finer vibrations of the Higher World)* that are being revealed to you, the information may be relayed to you in many different forms such as symbols, signs, images, analogies, synchronicities etc.

If you do not let a single day go by without being still; tuning into the World of Light, and employing full beam concentration, something holy inside you will be touched and The Light will shine through. The Gifts of Spirit that you have will gradually be enhanced; new ones will be gained, and previous powers that were lost will be opened up again. While you are meditating, you may even be able to witness something that will be happening, in connection with the Great Event, before it manifests on the physical plane.

The information about the Great Event, that is in this book, means that not only will you be ready when the Great Event occurs, you will also have gained insight into the level of spiritual development that will be required when the next cycle of Life on Earth begins, for life will be lived at a higher evolved level as it once was on Atlantis. No matter what will be taking place in the Outer World, when the Great Event occurs, if you go within and meditate, you will feel calm and peaceful inside because of the understanding that you will have gained about the New Dawn of The Light in the World, Atlantis Rising, and the enhanced relationship that will manifest with The Almighty One.

Impressions about The Divine can be fleeting when you first start meditating. They need to be grasped hold of tightly immediately they emerge. Each detail, no matter how small, is pertinent and if its significance is not understood at the time, it will be later on when more knowledge has been gained.

Scepticism about what is being made known to you through clairvoyance, clairaudience, claircognisance etc. can limit your spiritual development. As Saint Teresa of Avila explained in her memoir, what is experienced is so far above the level of our earthly understanding that there is no way that we could invent such things. In his book, *Of Water and The Spirit*, Malidoma Patrice Some, said much the same thing. He maintained that nothing can be imagined that is not already there in the Inner World and that your mind is a receiver. It cannot imagine what does not exist.

Until you let go of any preconceptions that you have and meditate on the knowledge that is given to you with an open mind, your progress will be slow. It is, however, wise to be cautious until the level of your resonance with the Gifts of Spirit grows and even then, it is best to always start and finish each meditation with an affirmation such as this one:-

I AM POWERFULLY PROTECTED BY THE DIVINE LIGHT OF SPIRITUAL PROTECTION WHICH FLOWS THROUGH MY WHOLE BEING AND SURROUNDS MY WHOLE BEING SO I TRULY UNDERSTAND WHAT IS REVEALED TO ME AT ALL TIMES.

A willingly opened receptive heart is essential. What is revealed while you are 'in the Spirit' always needs to be viewed with the 'eye of your heart' and so that you can focus on the higher perspective of the vision, your heart needs to be filled with Divine Love and Peace.

Meditation can provide many benefits and there are various ways in which the meditative state can be entered into easily. One of the methods is to start the process by taking a long steady look at an inspirational image. Marion Lawrence's Spirit Art Cards have been included in this book to help you in this regard. If you soften your gaze, and let the colours flowing through the landscape carry you through the 'revolving door' and into the World of Light, before you begin reading each of the chapters in this book, when you come to explore what I have written about Atlantis, you will be able to do so with a new-found level of rapport.

When my Spiritual Director made me aware that it was time to write a report about what I had learned regarding the preparations for Atlantis to re-emerge on the physical plane, he asked me to include a detailed account of my past lives in which there was a connection with Atlantis. This is to shed light on why I am in possession of this knowledge about Atlantis and to demonstrate how our past lives can have an effect on our present lifetime. As a result, you will be able to view the Atlantean Mystery on a different level, from a different time, at a different angle and in a different place and when you reach the end of this book, you will also know a little more about someone who originally came from the Atlantean Race.

THE ACOLYTE

CRYSTAL CITIES OF ATLANTIS

*Let us remember to always work
for the highest good of all.
Concerned with love and light,
the jewel of Atlantis is knowledge.*

MARION LAWRENCE

Many moons ago, I was an Acolyte of The Priest of Atlantis and I was in The Temple of The Sun Disc preparing for my final initiation. My name was, ISHKA RINZA.[1] ISHKA was the title given to an Acolyte. It was only awarded if the Third Eye, the Fourth Eye and the Fifth Eye had opened.

The Three Spiritual Eyes

The Third Eye was called the 'Sun Disc.' (*Very many moons later it came to be associated with the 'Son' and Christ Consciousness.*) When this eye opened, a flash of electric blue light was emitted from the area between the eyebrows.

The Fourth Eye was known as the 'Moon Disc.' When it opened, a flash of silvery white light mixed with electric blue light was emitted from the centre of the forehead. The combined power of the Sun and Moon Discs, working in harmony with the Heart Chakra, meant that the focus was adjusted correctly so the intensity of the radiance of the Light in the Fifth Eye could be tolerated.

---

[1] I^SH>KA> (i^ (as in 'it')–shhh-kahhh (sounds like 'car'))
RI^NZA> (ri^n (rhymes with 'fin')-zahhh)

The Fifth Eye was called the 'Star.' Once this eye opened, a flash of lilac and purple light mixed with electric blue light was emitted from the top of the forehead. It was associated with sight of the Angelic Realms and beyond. When the multi-rayed Star of the Holy Spirit was witnessed, it heralded that the eye had fully opened and the radiance of The Light of SHI, The Source of All Wisdom, was going to be experienced. Attunement to the 11th Ray of the Star was the highest level of attunement that could be attained at that time.

Eleven Rays of the Multi-rayed Star

The inner circle of the Star consisted of the five rays of the golden illuminating Light of Christ Consciousness. The six rays surrounding the inner circle related to the silver ascension Light of the Holy Spirit.

The 1st Ray was the Ray of Attunement. It enabled the process for an Enhanced Relationship with The Almighty to be witnessed, which in turn enabled the understanding of the Divine that had been attained to be increased, and new knowledge about The Divine to be assimilated. The Ray contained many shades of shimmering green light mixed with gold light. The hues of the green light were of a very high vibration and they enabled attunement to the other rays to take place.

The 2nd Ray was the Ray of Holiness. Within it many ethereal shades of white light, mixed with gold light could be seen. Once a certain level of holiness had been attained, this ray enabled a higher level of harmony, with what was being witnessed, to be opened up.

The 3rd Ray was the Ray of Wisdom. It contained many shades of gold light. It was essential that Divine Wisdom was possessed as the Ray enabled the dance of the particles to be seen, and it was vital that this knowledge was not used for destructive purposes.

The 4th Ray was the Ray of the Power of Absolute Love. It contained numerous hues of pink, lilac and purple light mixed with gold light and enabled the glories of Absolute Love to be witnessed.

The Power of the 5th Ray enabled the Vibrations of the Holy Spirit to be seen. The Ray contained many shades of sparkling silver light mixed with gold light.

The Power of the 6th Ray was that it shone light on the mysteries and what was witnessed as a result, enabled progress to a Higher Evolved Level of Consciousness to be quickened. The Ray only emitted silver light, as did the rest of the rays, although in increasing intensity.

The Power of the 7th Ray enabled the Inner World to be witnessed continuously. Attunement to this Ray was an essential part of the process for an enhanced relationship with The Almighty One to come about.

The 8th Ray was the Ray of the Lightning Strike. Witnessing a Strike could mean the retrieval of lost powers; the enhancement of existing powers, or the opening up of new powers.

The Light of the 9th Ray pierced the heart so that the True Reality could be witnessed.

The Power of the 10th Ray enabled a trajectory of the Divine Plan to be witnessed - the increase of the Divine Force in the Spark.

The Power of the Light of the 11th Ray enabled many more of the gradations of The Light to be witnessed so attunement to the Divine Plan and the ongoing work of the Holy Spirit could take place. It also quickened awareness of the Presence of The Almighty One so the radiance of The Light of SHI could be witnessed as fully as possible while in the human form.

The 11th Ray Initiation

I had been attuned to all of the rays except the 11th Ray. The final initiation, if it was successful, would mean that I would become a member of The Sisterhood and Brotherhood of The Eleventh Ray.

The Priest of Atlantis was going to carry out my attunement to the 11th Ray. He had gone to the Holy of Holies to retrieve the pure white Holy Vessel that was kept in the shrine there. The Holy Receptacle was used in the Initiation Ceremony as it represented the Temple's ethos of pure consciousness. An earthquake had split the shrine in two, but miraculously the Holy Vessel had not been damaged.

The Priest had, what was called, 'a heavenly face.' This was because below each of his physical eyes there were three horizontal lines. Although the lines were on The Priest's face, they were like the lines on the palms of our hands in that they were on his face at birth and each line had a meaning.

The first line below each of The Priest's eyes signified Holiness; the second line was the mark of Wisdom, and the third line signified the level of Power that The Priest possessed – the Power of Absolute Love.

The Priest's name was, EAXZOS.[1] It meant, 'One Called by God to Increase Humanity's Attunement to The Light.' His name was written as follows:-

---

[1] EAXZ>O^S> (ee-ay-x-zzz-o^ (as in 'on')-sss)

As The Priest came towards me, I noticed that he was clothed in a magnificent gold garment and on his head there was a tall gold headdress that consisted of three arches of gold light.

It had been foretold that one who had dwelt on Atlantis would be known as a Great Soul of Light Supreme and as a result of seeing The Priest's apparel, I knew with absolute certainty that The Priest was a Great Soul of Light Supreme. 1 bowed and uttered this salutation:

"Son of The Light, EAXZOS, I greet you.
Beloved One of The Almighty, your name is holy.
To you will be given honour, glory and praise."

The Priest gently said:-

"Dear Soul of Light, you continue to be amazed at all that has been revealed to you, but you have the capacity to receive more knowledge. The learnedness that you have attained about The Light of SHI is going to be increased because you are now able to assimilate a more profound level of resonance with The Divine.

"When I awaken you it will mean that the first part of your initiation will have taken place and your resonance with The Divine will have been intensified to the level where you will be able to hear the sound of The Name of The Almighty One."

The Priest held up the Holy Vessel and drew my attention to the insignia of The Sisterhood and Brotherhood of The Eleventh Ray that was on the Holy Receptacle. An eleven rayed star had been etched on the Holy Vessel. The star had six outer rays and five inner rays and in the centre of the inner rays there was a rose quartz crystal symbolising Absolute Love.

As I gazed at the crystal, the 'eye of my heart' opened and an overwhelming feeling of Divine Love filled the energy centre (*chakra*) of my heart when I looked up at The Priest; for I was now able to see that his aura was filled with the beautiful unworldly hues of the energy of Absolute Love.

The Priest pointed the middle finger *(the fire finger)* on his right hand at me. A gold beam was emitted from his finger. It touched my Third Eye and fully opened it; a second beam touched my Throat Chakra and fully opened that energy centre, and a third beam touched my Heart Chakra and fully opened that energy centre too.

Three powerful lightning strikes of the Divine Energy of the Holy Spirit followed in each of the chakras. I was encompassed by a force that was similar to a whirlwind and before I lost consciousness, I saw a spiral of silver light flowing down my central light column.

The 'whirlwind' had gone when I was awoken by The Priest tapping my Third Eye, Throat and Heart Chakras. This was to check that they were fully operating on the frequency that would enable me to see what he would be seeing, hear what he would be hearing, and to make sure that my heart was filled with the level of Absolute Love that would mean that I would be able to assimilate what he was going to experience. He said:-

"Dear One of Soul Sight, the light of the silver spiral is so fine that it is not always possible for there to be attunement to its vibration, but this part of your initiation was successful."

This meant that once the final part of my initiation had taken place, not only would my Third Eye be fully opened, my Fourth Eye and Fifth Eye would be fully opened too indicating that my consciousness would have ascended to the level where I could be called an ISHIKA.[1] This title signified membership of The Sisterhood and Brotherhood of The Eleventh Ray.

The Sign

The Priest held the Holy Vessel above his head and began rotating. As the rotations became faster, his robe of gold light expanded and he looked up.

I looked up too and saw that the Sign of the Holy Spirit had appeared above The Priest. My heart was filled with joy and thanksgiving that I had been gifted with the ability to be able to witness the wondrous sight of the multi-rayed, multicoloured Star.

Out of the circular opening in the centre of the inner circle of the Star a rapid stream of Holy Light was being emitted, and as it poured down into the Holy Receptacle, I was able to hear the Sacred Vibrations of the Holy Spirit that were resonating in The Priest's Heart Chakra.

---

[1] I^SH>IKA> (i^ (as in 'it')–shhh-ee-kahhh (sounds like 'car'))

The Sacred Vibrations

The first sound was a series of gentle (eye-eye-eye) bleeps:-

'I – I – I'

Next there was a harmonious humming sound like an elongated 'm':-

'mmmmmmm'

It was followed by the sound of a mighty rushing wind:-

'roo-oo-oo-shhhhh'

Then there was a high pitched sound like the 'ting' of a small bell:-

'in**ggg**'

It was followed by a clicking sound:-

'k-tahhh'

Then came the buzzing sound of the Lightning Strike

'zzzerr'

and the seven symbols of The Name of SHI were burnt on to the Holy Vessel. They represented the forces that were associated with the sounds that had been emitted. The Almighty One's Name was written as follows:-

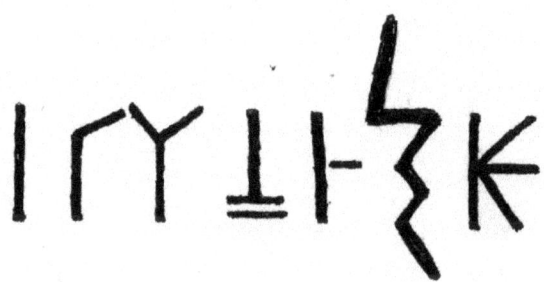

The last symbol was a whistling sound that was known as the 'Breeze of Spirit.' It wrapped round all the other sounds so that the power of the forces within The Name would not harm me or The Priest; for it is the power of these elusive sounds that holds the Universe together.

Now that I knew The Name of SHI, it meant that not only had I attained pure consciousness and my attunement to the 11th Ray had been successfully completed, most importantly of all, my relationship with The Almighty One had been enhanced. This was only possible if The Name of SHI was known.

The Destruction of Atlantis

I was aware that my Initiation was the final one that The Priest was going to carry out on Atlantis, and I saw that the white Cosmic Cloud Craft had appeared that was going to take him to a Higher Dimension.

(This mode of transport was used by The Priest in another lifetime as recorded in Acts 1:9-11 NKJV. 'Now when He had spoken these things, while they watched, He was taken up, and a cloud received Him out of their sight. And while they looked steadfastly toward Heaven as He went up, behold, two men stood by them in white apparel, who said, "Men of Galilee, why do you stand gazing up into Heaven? This same Jesus, who was taken up from you into Heaven, will so come in like manner as you saw Him go into Heaven."')

Before he entered the vehicle, The Priest gave me the Holy Vessel. I held on to the Holy Receptacle as tightly as possible, for seawater was engulfing the Temple now.

I did not want the Holy Vessel to fall into the hands of someone who knew how to 'read' 'The Name' either, as I was aware that some Atlanteans would not use the power that went with knowing 'The Name' responsibly or wisely.

Such power can be beneficial or destructive and a significant number of Atlanteans had misused the powers that they had been given. They were known as the 'Sons of Belial.' One of their experiments with the power of sound had contributed to Atlantis disappearing beneath the waves, and so it was that when my physical body sank into the Ocean of Darkness so did the Holy Vessel too and, for a very long time, The Name of SHI, The Almighty One, was hidden from humanity.

THE SCRIBE

PART I
The Novice

THE SPHINX

Riddle of humanity;
key to the mysteries;
look beyond what you see.

MARION LAWRENCE

Consciousness is a spark from The Almighty One and it never dies. One of the lives that I experienced after Atlantis was destroyed was an incarnation, in Egypt, as a male Scribe, called NYYATU[1]. The Priest of Atlantis was there at that time. He oversaw my upbringing and when I was twelve years old, The Priest enrolled me on the Course for Scribes at the Mystery School that Thoth, The Atlantean, had started. Before I began the course, The Priest took me to a special monument that was in the grounds of the School.

The Atlantean Sphinx

Many advanced Atlantean souls had migrated to Egypt just before The Fall and they had brought the Sphinx with them. This statue had been commissioned by Thoth to honour a Being who had been revered due to the advanced paranormal abilities that she possessed. One of her spiritual gifts was the ability to shine a light on the darkness.

[1] NYYATU (nigh-yahhh-too)

She was clothed in a silver garment signifying the connection that she had with the Moon, as well as the Moon Disc (*Fourth Eye*), for she had a great deal more knowledge about The Light of SHI than any of the Atlanteans. This was because her heart was tuned to the optimal frequency of the Divine Vibration of Absolute Love, The Source of All Wisdom.

The head of a cat had been placed on the statue to represent her beautiful face and eyes which had a feline quality to them. A long tail had been added to the back of the upright body of the Atlantean Sphinx to portray the balance and agility that she had in all matters. Her grace and speed of movement was definitely feline in nature, and she outshone the Atlanteans in every way because of the powers that she possessed. She was dignified, mysterious, very, very wise, and a skilled negotiator.

(The head that was placed over Thoth's body in Egypt was that of an ibis. The Egyptians considered that of all the birds, the ibis was the wisest. Thoth's Egyptian name was Tehuti. The oldest name for the ibis was 'tehu' and 'ti' was a title of respect for one who was in possession of the powers, qualities and abilities of an ibis. Thoth had several other abilities attributed to him, one of which was Messenger/Scribe to the Gods. This was because he brought knowledge about the alphabet, writing, The Mysteries, and many other things as well.)

Before we went into Thoth's School, The Priest told me that when the Atlantean had arrived in Egypt, he chose a special place to hide knowledge about the Great Event of

Atlantis re-emerging. It included details of the enhanced relationship with The Almighty One that would flourish again in the New Dawn of The Light in the World.

The Seven Levels of Preparation

As I went through the two columns at the entrance of the majestic white building that was Thoth's School, I saw that there was a large white circle on the floor of the hallway. The Priest told me that once seven levels of preparation and three initiations had been completed satisfactorily, the title of Scribe of The Eleventh Ray would be awarded to me.

I was then made aware that Thoth was also an Alchemist, but instead of learning how to turn base metal/lead into gold, each level of preparation would be achieved through the process of the Alchemy of Meditation until my consciousness was refined so that it could be fully attuned to the gold light of Wisdom.

The First Level

During the first level of preparation I sat in the centre of the white circle every day and meditated. The white circle symbolised the purification of consciousness, through the removal of dross, so The Light could shine through.

Behind the circle was a shaft of light and although I faced the entrance to the School, when I sat down in the circle I was immediately aware that there was a Presence in the shaft of light behind me.

One day, after many, many months of meditating in the white circle, I saw a pair of subtle hands next to mine. They signified that when I was a Scribe, I would be guided so that the purity of the knowledge that I had access to would be maintained as I was recording the message or information. I had been able to see the hands because my Third Eye had opened and this meant that I was ready to go to the hall on the next level.

The Second Level

There was also a white circle on the floor of the hall on the second level and the shaft of light was behind the circle as before. The circle was, however, surrounded by small diamonds. After I had sat in the centre of the circle meditating for awhile, The Priest gave me a book to study. It was called *Book of Thoth* and it had a silver coating on the cover that looked like liquid mercury.

On the first page there was a gold vertical zigzag symbolising a lightning strike. It served as a reminder that all the alchemical knowledge that was obtained was to be used wisely.

On the next page there was a diagram of a pyramid. The Priest told me that this level of preparation was concerned with the initiations, and that they would be taking place in the three pyramids at Giza.

From the base to the top of the diagram of the pyramid, there were horizontal rows of symbols. Once I placed the first overlay that accompanied the page on top of the diagram, vertical lines appeared over the diagram making a grid so that every one of the alchemical symbols was contained in a box.

When I placed an overlay over the first overlay the symbols in the vertical column at the centre of the pyramid were converted into the image of a gold wire that went straight down the whole of the column.

A third overlay revealed that a silver spiral went round the gold wire and both the wire and the spiral extended beyond the top of the pyramid. The Priest explained that together they formed an aerial.

The fourth overlay converted the symbols in the horizontal column in the centre of the pyramid into the formula for the white substance that coated the whole of the outside of the pyramid. The Priest described how the covering enabled images to be shown on the outside of the pyramid. They were transmitted through the aerial by the Inter-Galactic Council's twelve Elders who had a special resonance with our galaxy and it also enabled whoever meditated in the pyramid to make contact with the Elders and receive information about the ascension of the Human Race.

The fifth overlay highlighted the box at the base of the vertical column that went through the centre of the pyramid and the box at the top of that column. The boxes at the far ends of the horizontal column that went through the centre of the structure were highlighted too. The Priest asked me to tell him what I was able to 'read' about the diagram from the fifth overlay. Straightaway, I was able to inform The Priest that I could see that a diamond filled the pyramid as follows:-

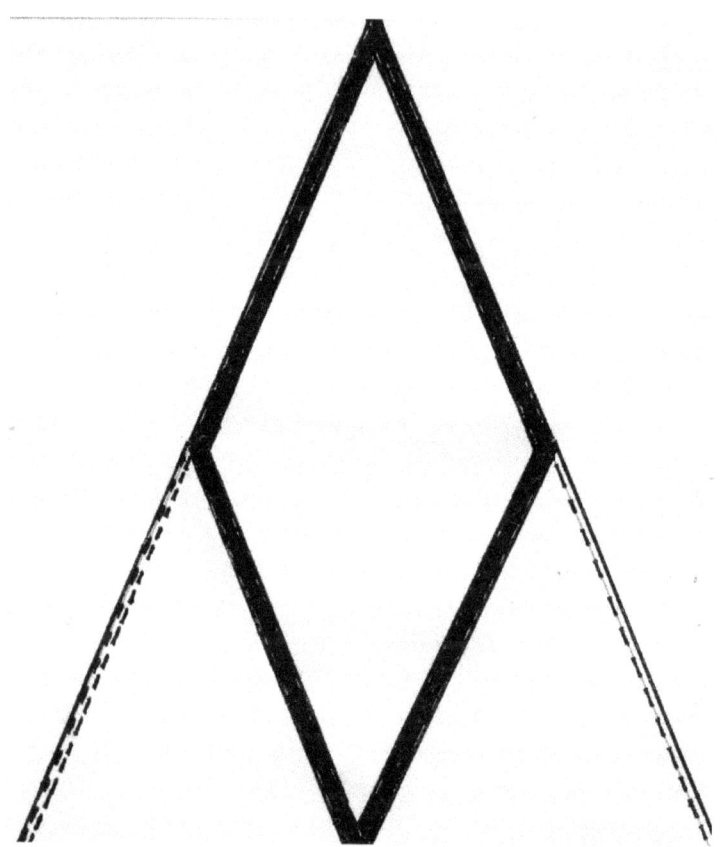

I was then informed by The Priest that at the peak of the Atlantean Age, Atlanteans had the ability to maximise the power of crystals and gemstones and that after diamonds had been mined, they were activated so that they produced sufficient light to generate a covering of higher frequency light over the whole of Atlantis.

A sparkling diamond was then placed in my hands and the Priest asked me to meditate on its properties.

As instructed, I held the diamond against my Third Eye first. I saw numerous rays being emitted from the diamond in all directions and as I watched those rays connecting with the rays coming from the diamonds surrounding the white circle that I was sitting in, I realised that they had formed a grid over and around me.

The Priest told me to hold the diamond against my Throat Chakra next and commune with the gemstone. I learned that this diamond was a receiver and transmitter. In other words, it had been specially primed for use by a Scribe.

Finally, The Priest directed me to hold the diamond against my Heart Chakra and as I gently stroked the diamond and communed with its energy, I felt the 'screen/eye of my heart' being opened. A stream of diamond light flowed across the screen and I understood that all the knowledge that I received from then on would be screened by the eye of my heart. The subtle hands then appeared round my hands signalling that this level of preparation had been completed.

The Third Level

The white circle on the floor of the hall on the third level had a gold circle on top of it and in the centre of the gold circle there was a very small circle. I recognised the gold circle as being the alchemical symbol for gold, the sun and also the gold light of Wisdom.

I sat down in the centre of the gold circle and as soon as I closed my eyes and started meditating I saw gold 'Sun' light flowing down from my Third Eye to my Heart Chakra. As I basked in the warmth of the 'Sun' light, I was attuned to the frequency of the subtle body on which the higher harmonies of Divine Peace and Love could be heard. They elicited in me a feeling of utter bliss and I felt reluctant to leave this level when the subtle hands appeared signifying it was time for me to go up to the next level.

The Fourth Level

Over the white circle on the floor of the hall on the fourth level was a silver circle. In the centre of this circle there was the symbol of an eleven rayed star and a rose quartz crystal had been placed in the centre of the image of the star.

The Priest said, "Dear One of Soul Sight, the symbol of this star holds special significance. You have reached the level where a Luminary of The Light will appear and give you instruction about its connection to a multi-rayed Star. To digest the knowledge will take time, but perseverance will enable you to fully assimilate the information that you will be given, as knowledge that you possessed in a previous lifetime, about the multi-rayed Star, will eventually come back to you."

I was asked by The Priest to face the shaft of light from then on when I was meditating. I sat down and as I gazed at the pink quartz crystal, I was overwhelmed by a feeling of love that was so powerful that it seemed to me that I had never experienced anything like it before and then the eye of my heart opened and I saw on its screen a multi-rayed Star.

When I looked up I could see that in the shaft of light there was a Being who was surrounded by green light indicating the fertile infinite mind of an Immortal Being. I realised that one of the powers that I had once possessed, which had now been reactivated, was the ability to see the whole of the subtle form of a Being of Light. As I gazed in awe at the Being whose subtle hands I had only had sight of previously, I knew that I was seeing one of Thoth's guises. He communicated with me through telepathy and I heard him say:-

"Dear One, the Light is shining brightly in your soul. The passage of time has not dimmed its glow. You have consumed the knowledge that you have been given with enthusiasm and have worked diligently at your studies, so my Presence has been revealed to you.

"Your Sun Disc *(Third Eye)* and your Moon Disc *(Fourth Eye)* have opened; the illuminating power of the Sun Disc and the ascension power of the Moon Disc have combined; the eye of your heart has also opened, and, as a result, you have seen on the screen the multi-rayed Star. You can compare it to a star in the sky if you wish, but it is much more than that. Behind it is the Power that rules the waves of consciousness, emits the light that comes through the Sun and Moon Discs, and talks to you via the Breeze/Holy Spirit. A qualified Messenger/Scribe needs to be able to rise to the domain of the Holy Spirit so that direct contact with The Divine can be experienced. Messages or knowledge will then be acquired and the Messenger/Scribe will be tasked with making the information known to their earthly companions."

Thoth held out his hands and as I went towards him, the Atlantean activated in my aura the silver light of a Messenger/Scribe. I was then able to go up the shaft of light to the next level.

The Fifth Level

On the floor of the hall on the fifth level there was a large silver circle and before I sat down in the centre of the circle and began meditating, I received this blessing from Thoth:-

"Dear One, may you surrender to this level of freedom from the limitations of the human mind with joy; may your wings of light carry you to dimensions that you knew many moons ago, and may your understanding of The Profound become much greater."

As soon as I entered the meditative state I saw that the silver vehicle of the Messenger/Scribe was waiting for me. It meant that every day I could travel to different dimensions, higher heavens, and radiant realms and so every day, I embarked on a glorious adventure; every day I learned something new and exciting, and every day brought a new-found sense of wonder.

One day, the vehicle took me to the base of an extremely high cliff. Light cascaded down from the top of the cliff into a large lake and as I bathed in the lake, a feeling of deep peace came over me. While I was relaxing, I became aware that in a cave nearby there was a fabulous crystal that had special powers. It did not take me long to find the cave as the entrance to it was illuminated by green light. Deep in the cave was a huge gemstone and as I gazed at the crystal I was entranced by its beauty. I would have liked to stay in the cave longer, but I returned to the School as soon as I heard The Priest calling me.

The Priest was waiting for me in the hall and explained that because of the discovery that I had made, it meant that I was ready to go to the sixth floor.

As we were going up the shaft of light, The Priest explained that on another level, when the waterfall of emotions are calmed in the tranquil lake of light that appears during meditation, a reflection can be seen of the cave of the heart. The treasures that are stored in the cave can only be viewed when sufficient preparation has been undertaken so that the knowledge that will be gained about them will be able to be assimilated.

The Sixth Level

On a stand in the hall of the sixth level there was a magnificent emerald gemstone that was like the crystal that I had seen in the cave. The Priest asked me to tell him what came to mind as I gazed at the emerald. I told The Priest that the words, Love, Loyalty, and Longevity had come to me.

The Priest explained that Absolute Love, the Source of All Wisdom, was the foundation on which the School was built.

With regards to Loyalty, he made me aware that now that the level of my insight had been streamlined, I would be able to assimilate what was going to be opened out to me by Thoth. This meant that I would be required to swear an Oath of Allegiance to The Order of the Human Messengers of The Divine.

I learned that Longevity related to the connection with Thoth being renewed from age to age and at a pre-ordained time, the knowledge that a qualified Messenger/Scribe was to make known would be divulged to them.

The hall was bathed in beautiful green light now. It signified that Thoth was in the hall. I sat down and as I started meditating on all that I had learned so far about the Alchemy of Meditation, I found Thoth's light very soothing. I felt happy about swearing the Oath of Allegiance and ready to form an eternal bond with Thoth.

The Seventh Level

I stood up and The Priest accompanied me up the shaft of light to the level where the ceremony was going to take place. Once we were in the hall of the seventh level, the process was started at once.

The Salute of The Order of Messengers

The Priest showed me how to perform the special salute first of all. It consisted of three movements.

The first movement was to raise the right arm. It was placed in front of the centre of the chest with the right hand resting on the forehead. The palm of the hand faced outwards with the fingers and thumb touching and bent over in a horizontal position to represent the Serpent of

The Source of All Wisdom with its head in the position that indicated that it was about to strike.

(Although this was originally reserved as a salute by The Order of Messengers to The Source of All Wisdom, it was adopted by Pharaohs and took the form of a depiction of a cobra being attached to a headband and positioned over the area of the Third Eye.)

The second movement was to cross both arms over the chest diagonally.

The third movement was to place the back of the right hand horizontally over the forehead.

The Oath of The Order of Messengers

When I had perfected the movements, I repeated the words of The Oath after The Priest had said them. They were as follows:-

"I do solemnly swear an Oath of Allegiance to The Order of Human Messengers of The Divine.

"I do solemnly swear that I will share the messages that I am given with my earthly companions so that they are prepared for the Great Event.

"I do solemnly swear that as a Messenger of Peace I will use the powers granted to me wisely and always from my heart.

"I do solemnly swear that I will continue doing all that I can to expand the Peace and Divine Love that are in my heart.

"I place my trust wholeheartedly in The Light."

The Emerald Tablet

To commemorate the swearing of The Oath, The Priest placed an Emerald Tablet in my hands. It has been said that there is nothing new under the sun. The original tablet, 'engineered' by the Atlantean's advanced alchemical expertise with regards to crystals, consisted of a circuit board of four rows of chips from Thoth's Emerald.

The circuit board was activated by touching, 'swiping,' or holding down the chips in a certain way. Bright green light was emitted from each of the crystals that were used when a symbol was put into the tablet. Images then appeared on the screen of the eye of the heart and messages could be received via the screen too. Each row consisted of four small emerald chips as follows:-

The Priest then gave me instructions on how to activate the tablet. First of all, I was told to touch the second emerald on the right of the top row. It started flashing and a series of alchemical symbols appeared on the screen. Next I was asked to 'swipe' the emeralds on the third horizontal row from right to left. Then I 'swiped,' the emeralds, from left to right, in a diagonal line from the emerald on the left of the third row up to the second emerald on the right of the top row. Finally, I 'swiped' down from the second emerald on the right of the top row to the second emerald on the right of the fourth row to make a symbol that was like the number four as follows:-

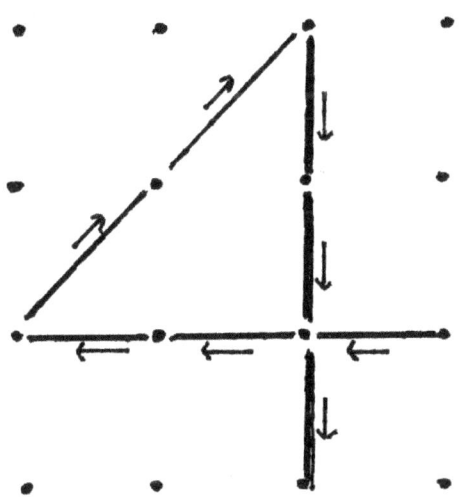

As a result, I received the following message:-

This tablet has now been programmed so that greater depth can be established in the work that you will be doing.

The Priest then asked me to hold down the emeralds on either end of the first row as hard as I was able to. A vertical line appeared on the circuit board from the top row to the bottom row in the centre of the tablet and a horizontal row appeared across the centre. A button emerged in the centre of the tablet as follows:-

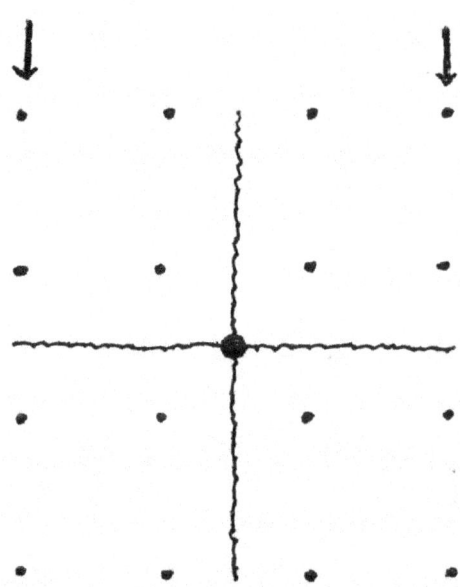

I was told to push down the button in the centre of the tablet and as I did so, the sound of a siren started being emitted from the tablet. The Priest explained that this symbol signified Peril. After I had meditated on this symbol and its uses, The Priest showed me another symbol as follows:-

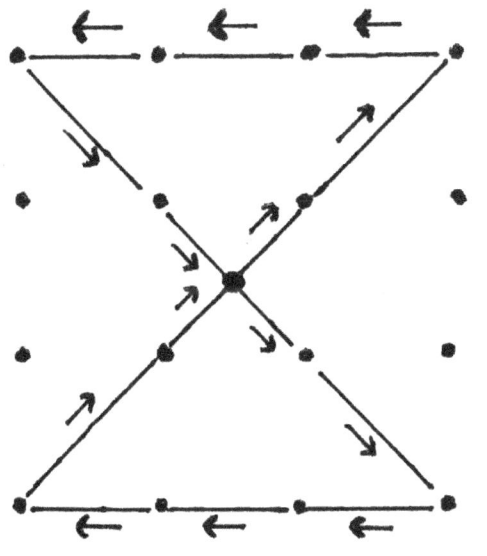

This symbol represents the earthly cycle of time. In other words, it was used when it was time to bring something into being. *(In Egypt, Thoth was known as the Moon God and the Moon was regarded as the measurer of time, hence one of Thoth's titles was 'The Measurer.')*

Once I had memorised this symbol, The Priest asked me to push down on the four emeralds in the centre of the tablet at the same time. A large button emerged around the four emeralds as follows:-

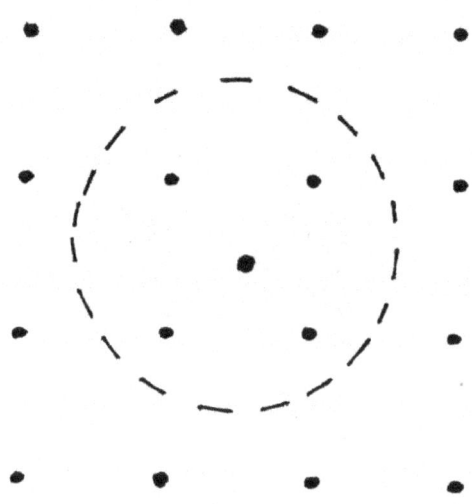

Next, The Priest asked me to press the left and right sides of the large button at the same time and the powerful image of the multi-rayed Star, the Eternal Compass of the Holy Spirit, appeared on the screen of the eye of my heart.

The emeralds on both ends of the top row and both ends of the bottom row, as well as the four emeralds in the centre of the tablet and the button in the middle of them immediately lit up as follows:-

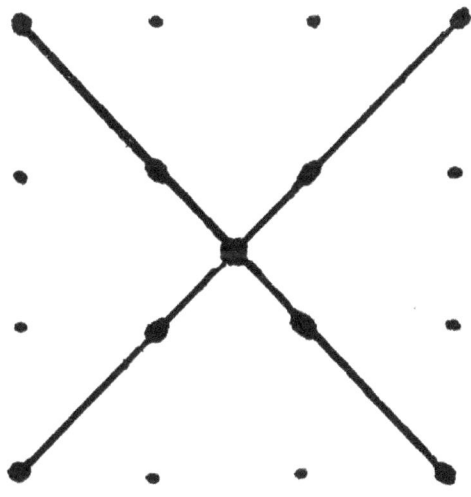

Confirmation was then given to me that I had satisfactorily completed the first part of the Course and that it was time for the next part of the Course to be brought into being as this message appeared on the screen:-

'ADVANCE'

A door swung open and The Priest took me along a passageway that led to the Great Pyramid of Giza as that was where I would have to demonstrate that I would be ready to participate in the rise, when it was inchoate, of the next Atlantean Superstate.

THE SCRIBE

PART II
The Initiate

JOURNEY THROUGH THE LABYRINTH

*Journey through the Labyrinth
of your Soul's journey and
come out of the other
side a new you,
a new step
ahead.*

MARION LAWRENCE

On the way to the Great Pyramid, The Priest informed me that the first test was about overcoming fear. If I was able to complete the test, a Gift of Spirit that I possessed in a previous lifetime would be re-activated and insight would be gained about something that had been hidden in plain sight.

The Priest told me to go to the King's Chamber; remove my clothing and tie the short white 'apron' that I would find in the chamber round my waist, and meditate while lying in the sarcophagus there.

The First Initiation

As soon as I started meditating, the Great Dragon appeared above me. The legend of the Great Dragon appearing during an initiation was well known and as it overshadowed the sarcophagus with its massive wings, I felt very afraid. Fire was coming from the Dragon's nostrils, its slimy scales were repulsive, and its claws were outstretched as though it was going to grab me.

I was, however, soon able to overcome my fear by using a technique that I had learned during the preparatory part of the Course. This entailed asking the Radiant Light of SHI to protect me and envisaging a circle of pure white light continuously revolving round the whole of my being.

Now that I was no longer terrified of the Dragon, it changed its 'tune.' It even sang an exquisite song to me and during the song I learned that the Dragon was the guardian of priceless treasures, higher wisdom, and supernatural powers. The Dragon left me in peace after that.

A powerful green current then started flowing through me. It was a pleasant sensation and once the flow stopped I sat up. I noticed that a partition on the right side of the chamber had been opened. Thoth's Emerald was in the compartment and I realized that the Atlantean had programmed the gemstone to emit the current.

When I climbed out of the sarcophagus I was aware that it signified that I had been reborn and I felt energised and ready to take on any other challenges I might encounter.

Thoth was standing next to the emerald and my attention was drawn to the crown that the Atlantean was wearing. It encapsulated Thoth's title, *'Ancient of Days/Measurer of Time*;' for the crown portrayed the crescent moon and the sun as follows:-

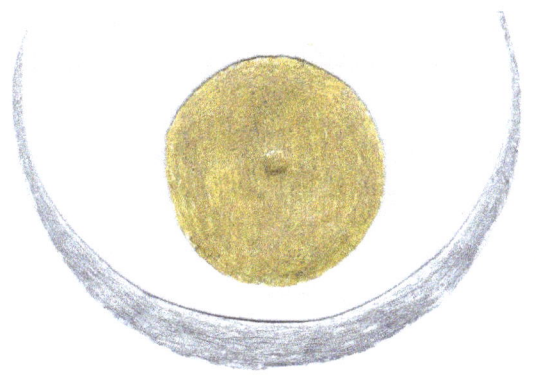

I saluted Thoth in the way that I had been taught, and the Atlantean responded by saying:-

"Dear One of Soul Sight, the images that you will be seeing will be synchronised with the level of your understanding. They will bring to light a future happening. Trust in your understanding of what will be revealed to you. Enmesh the images in your heart, for there you will find a great treasure. Devote time after each initiation to appraising what has ensued and record the wisdom that you gain on your emerald tablet."

The Gift of Foreknowledge

A large hand was placed on my forehead and instantly a vision occurred in which I was sitting on a sandy beach. I became aware that the Breeze of Spirit was wafting around me.

On the horizon, there was a huge silvery-gold disc that looked like a sun that was just starting to rise out of the water. A feeling of deep peace came upon me as I watched silvery-gold light flow across the waves in the form of a pathway.

In the distance I could see a dolphin leaping out of the water as though it was trying to get my attention and then I noticed that a silver tube like object with a pointed section at the front of it was travelling, at great speed, along the 'sun's' pathway towards the beach.

When the craft landed on the beach, I got into it and the vehicle set off over the waves. The dolphin travelled alongside the craft for awhile and then my Guide leapt out of the water making the clicking noise of the universal call sign, 'k-tahhh.'

A powerful beam of light came up from the seabed; a transparent canopy came forward from the back of the vehicle, and it dived down to a tunnel *(an underwater wormhole)*. As it went into the wormhole, the craft became the size of a silver bullet. The next thing I knew was that I was in another dimension and the vehicle was slowly going along a passageway.

The passageway kept on getting narrower and narrower but due to Atlantean technology the craft was able to change shape according to the environment that it had entered. Eventually, it emerged from the passageway and came to a halt outside a temple that was built into a rock face. It was known as *'The Treasury of Spiritual Knowledge.'*

The imposing structure had six columns on the ground level. On the next level of the facade, there were more columns and in a central position near the top of the temple/treasury there was a receptacle that looked like an urn. Although I realised that it was a replica of something that I had had a connection with, I could not recall why that was the case.

A white Cosmic Cloud Craft suddenly appeared over the temple and it dawned on me that it was something that could be classed as being hidden in plain sight; for it looked like a long cloud in the sky.

The Priest of Atlantis emerged from the vehicle first. Many Beings followed him and they walked along a path in single file. The path led to a mountain and when the Beings arrived there they all placed a symbol on the mountain.

There were two Beings standing on top of the mountain and once all the symbols were in place, a vertical channel of violet light opened up above the centre of the mountain. It came from a multi-faceted diamond and as the diamond started rotating, wings of rainbow light emerged from the jewel. A huge wave of light erupted from the hearts of the Beings and as they looked so happy, I gathered that they had been waiting a long time for this event to take place.

The vision faded and as soon as I was fully back in the pyramid, Thoth informed me that all the Beings who had emerged from the Cosmic Cloud Craft had originally come from Atlantis and that the symbols that they had placed on the mountain were symbols of peace. They signified that the various spiritual traditions that many of the Beings had founded after they migrated from Atlantis would become as One. The Atlanteans were rejoicing because the time had finally come for a veil to be removed. This meant that the mountain of spiritual inheritance that had originated in Atlantis could now be raised to a higher level thereby enabling what had been unseen to become visible.

Thoth made it clear to me that **by witnessing what had taken place, I had participated in the event**. The Atlantean reminded me to take to heart what I had been shown as it needed to be considered from a higher perspective.

Since it had been established that I had regained the Gift of Spirit, which I had had in a previous life, of being able to see far into the future, I was deemed to be ready to undergo the next initiation. The Measurer of Time told me that the Second Initiation would involve a special gift being attained; a special journey being undertaken, and two special rites taking place.

The Second Initiation

I was shown the entrance to the passageway that led to the second pyramid and was told that I was to make the journey along it on my own. The corridor was completely dark and I was concerned about what might be lying in wait for me as I went along the passageway so I asked for the protection of The Light of SHI. Instantly, a whirlwind of unearthly white light engulfed me. I was rapidly carried along the corridor and as I was deposited in a chamber in the second pyramid, I gave heartfelt thanks for the protection that I had received.

The Special Gift

It had been posited that the Atlantean High Priestess, Isis, was a virgin when she gave birth to the Sun God, Horus. When I entered the chamber I saw that The Priest was wearing the hawk headdress of Horus and Thoth was wearing the ibis headdress. On a stand, in the centre of the chamber, the *Book of Thoth* was open and as I stood between The Priest and Thoth, I was able to see that the heading at the top of the page said:-

THE TRANSFER OF ATTRIBUTES FROM AN OTHER SOURCE FOR THE REALIZATION OF A HIGHER LEVEL OF HARMONY WITH THE ALMIGHTY ONE

The Priest and Thoth turned round so that they were facing me. The 'Moon God of Wisdom and Divine Magic' was holding his fabulous emerald gemstone and he directed a beam from it through the side of my Solar

Plexus Chakra. The 'Sun God' sent the beam back to Thoth. This occurred three times causing the power of the beam to be increased each time. I heard The Priest say, "The level of power that has been switched on is so that you can appreciate the level of power that is in a hawk too" and suddenly I was flying high over the pyramid 'at One' with a hawk.

(The special gift of being able to shape-shift into a hawk was so this particular aspect of the Presence of The Almighty One could be experienced; for The Almighty One is the bird that you see, or the Beings that you behold. All are extensions of I AM THAT I AM. There is only one. I AM is all that is seen and all that is unseen. I AM is All That Is. I AM is within you and you are within I AM.

One of the attributes of the hawk is the ability to stay in the air for a long time and this is associated with being able to stay 'in the Spirit' for a long time. Another attribute is its powers of observation and this can be equated with the Eye of Horus, the spiritual eye.

Cultures around the world continue to use images of animals or birds, mythical or those still existing on Earth in shamanic rites not only to be in harmony with their essence, but also to be empowered by being attuned to their energies.)

The Special Flight

A wonderful feeling of freedom came over me as I soared higher and higher. I loved the purity of the air at the height that I was now able to go to; the strength of my wings, and the unlimited view of everything below me. The hawk swooped down low over the desert *(the barren place where past lives/events are not remembered)* and then headed out over the sea *(the waves of consciousness)* towards a huge silvery-gold disc.

The Breeze of Spirit wrapped round the hawk to protect us so that we were not burned as we got closer to the Atlantean Sun. As soon as a connection had been made in my Solar Plexus Chakra with this Sun, I heard The Priest say, "You will be able to reach inside yourself and draw out much more about your past lifetime in Atlantis now," and then I found myself back in the second pyramid.

The Second Chamber

The Priest and Thoth accompanied me along a corridor of white light and when we came to a partition, I was instructed to touch the symbol in the middle of the partition. I was very relieved when the partition slid open. Although I had been granted entry to the second chamber, it was in darkness except for a small flame. I was told to go and stand next to the flame.

Above the flame there was a circular object that was similar to a glitter ball. It started rotating and I was surrounded by fiery red light. It rose up as though it was going to engulf me and I had a vision of being burned alive. The rotation of the spotlight suddenly became faster and the fiery red light changed to blazing orange light. The heat was intense and I became aware that the crackling flames that encompassed me were getting higher and higher. The spotlight's rotation then became very fast; the orange light changed to yellow light; the flame in the centre of the chamber shot up through the ceiling, and a lightning strike occurred in my Solar Plexus Chakra.

When I came back to everyday consciousness I saw that I was standing in a circle that represented the Sun Disc. I realized that, like the hawk, I had flown close to the Sun without getting burned and that what had occurred had been my Baptism of Fire.

Beautiful hues of red, orange, yellow and gold light flowed round me now. I was relieved that the ordeal was over and pleased that I had resisted the urge to try and escape from what had seemed like a very real experience of being burned alive.

The Priest informed me that as a result of the lightning strike and my re-attunement to the energy of the Sun Disc, my Solar Plexus Chakra (*which is the Seat of Earthly Wisdom and the representation of the microcosmic sun*) would operate at a higher vibration. In addition, the connection between my Solar Plexus Chakra and my Third Eye Chakra *(the Seat of Higher Wisdom and the representation of the macrocosmic Sun)* would be enhanced.

When I turned round, I was now able to see that many Beings surrounded the image of the Sun Disc that was on the floor of the chamber. Due to the re-awakening in me of the Gift of Spirit of being able to recall past lives, I recognised some of the Beings. They were members of

The Sisterhood and Brotherhood of The Eleventh Ray and I had known them in a previous life in Atlantis when I was an Acolyte in the Temple of The Sun Disc. I went round the circle greeting all the Beings with the salute that The Priest had taught me and then I bowed, saluted Thoth and The Priest, and thanked them for preparing me for the Sun Disc Initiation.

Lastly, I gave thanks to SHI. I raised my arms as high above my head as they would go with my hands in prayer position at the Stargate Chakra and then I moved my hands down to my Crown, Third Eye, Throat and Heart Chakras before putting my hands, still in prayer position, but with my fingers pointing down, on my Solar Plexus Chakra symbolising the lightning strike of Divine Energy from the Holy Spirit coming down into my third major chakra.

The Third Initiation

The Priest took me to the third pyramid and told me that the final endurance test would involve more of my past life on Atlantis being revealed to me.

The chamber that we went into was filled with the unearthly electric green light that I had seen in the King's Chamber in the Great Pyramid. In the centre of the room there was a large gold Ankh.

The Priest explained that I was to gaze at the Ankh, while I was meditating, as it is the key that unlocks knowledge about Atlantis and I would then be re-attuned to the frequency on which Atlantis vibrated.

My Guide

I went into a deep level of meditation straightaway and saw that I was back at the beach where I had seen the dolphin leaping out of the water during the First Initiation. It was trying to show me something again.

The mode of transport that I had been given this time was a small boat with a sail. I got half way to the dolphin and then the current pulled me back to the beach.

The sea was calm when I started out again and I made good progress, but then the waves got choppy and I was not able to stay on course. Fortunately, I realized that I was losing my way and that I needed to ask my Guide for help. The dolphin telepathically transmitted this advice to me:-

"Dear One, now that the sail has been unfurled and all has been made ready for your journey back in time to the Atlantean World, let the Breeze of Spirit direct your course. Put your full trust in this Force. Remain alert and aware as you enter the Ocean of Light and know that there is nothing to fear about what you will see there. The vessel in which you have sailed has brought you to the place where something special will be unveiled. What is below will help you to realize how to relate to the elevation of Creation that is going to arise."

I had felt very anxious about returning to the site where the catastrophe had occurred. Although my anxiety had been holding me back, my desire to overcome the final challenge of the Course proved to be greater than my fear. It took all the strength that I had to do it; but I made the leap of faith and dived beneath the waves.

I went deeper and deeper and the dolphin accompanied me until I reached the 'seabed.' Directly in front of me was a white Temple that had a Sun Disc on top of the building. Above the entrance was the symbol of a leaping dolphin and in the centre of the symbol there was an emerald. *(Atlanteans considered their connection with dolphins to be of great importance. Dolphins were associated with Sirius and as messengers they communicated their knowledge and wisdom to the Atlanteans telepathically.)*

As soon as I entered the Temple I was overwhelmed by emotion as I could now remember the day that the Temple sank beneath the waves. I had not wanted to re-live that awful time, but it was obviously something that I had to do. After awhile, I ventured into the Holy of Holies and my sadness turned to joy; for I saw a vision of a large gold Ankh, and I knew that it would be the shrine in the Holy of Holies when The Temple of the Sun Disc was rebuilt on Risen Atlantis.

I realized then why the urn like vessel had seemed familiar to me when I arrived at the temple that I had been taken to during the First Initiation. It was a replica of the one that had stood on a shrine, in the Holy of Holies, when I was an Acolyte in The Temple of The Sun Disc many moons ago. Before the vision faded, I envisaged the Holy Vessel standing in the loop of the Ankh symbolising the restoration of pure consciousness.

The Visitor

When I arrived back in the third chamber of the pyramid, a Being was standing next to the Ankh there who I had not seen before. The Visitor was dressed in a silver all-in-one suit and he wore a helmet and shoes that had wings on them to denote his rank. I asked the Visitor who he was and if he came from The Light. The answer that I received was as follows:-

"My sign is the Crescent Moon. My abode is the Star. I light your path with my Love. I illuminate the Grace of The Way. I produce wisdom for you to digest. I open up mysteries that have lain hidden for ages. I mystically appear and disappear. I have been with you since time began.

"Who am I?

"I am The Messenger of the Gods."

The Presentation

The Messenger told me that I would always be a Scribe/Messenger as that was my true calling. Before The Messenger presented me with an Ankh, he reminded me of the eternal bond that I have with him. I held the

Ankh against my Heart Chakra and the Sacred Key lit up as though it had been electrified. A halo of rays appeared around the loop above the Tao cross of the Ankh signifying that its special powers had been activated by The Messenger.

The next gift that I was given came from The Priest. It was a special garment. At Heart Chakra level on the front of the robe was a sparkling eleven rayed star. In the centre of the star, there was a rose quartz crystal and I realised that the insignia of the Sisterhood and Brotherhood of The Eleventh Ray meant that my association with them would continue throughout all my lifetimes too.

The Temple

The final part of the Course was held at the nearby Temple. I went there with The Messenger and The Priest and it was obvious that the building was a place of worship for Atlanteans.

On the floor of the Temple there was a large circle and in it was the symbol of the re-emergence of Atlantis. The Benu bird *(Phoenix)* was standing on a straight three legged perch. Its wings were raised indicating that the bird was about to rise.

The Priest explained that the three legged perch signified that past, present and future are one. Everything is happening at the same time, but Human Beings are not able to assimilate all that is occurring at once so we divide it into past, present and future.

There are many different frequencies and numerous levels of consciousness. Past and future are just ways of seeing events from different angles: there is only the Eternal Now.

In order to absorb this knowledge, The Priest advised me to do a walking meditation round the symbol. From there I went up to God's Balcony in the Temple and received another startling revelation.

The Messenger was waiting for me on the balcony and I watched in amazement as he took off his all-in-one silver suit, his winged helmet and his shoes to reveal that he was an Extraterrestrial Being. Next, he opened up his Extraterrestrial exterior and I attained a very important insight: just as we are under our physical guises, Extraterrestrials are also Beings of Light.

THE WITNESS

PART I

The Alliance

GATEWAY TO ATLANTIS

*You have the Knowledge within.
It is time to remember.*

MARION LAWRENCE

Although many moons and many lifetimes have passed by since I was a Scribe/Messenger in Egypt, the connection is still strong with my Spiritual Director.

The Call

One morning recently, while I was meditating, I was delighted to receive the following call from The Priest of Atlantis. He said:-

"I am the way, the truth, and the Light, and you are very precious in my sight. Come to me, Beloved One, with love in your heart for all. This is a clarion wake-up call; for love is all that with you, you can take on the journey to the next level of Christ Consciousness that you are destined to make.

"Whither I go, you will be able to go. My feet will make fresh footsteps for you to follow so this time you will not be able to lose your way; for there cannot be any further delay. I am coming again to set you free so that you can ascend to the Realm of Higher Evolved Consciousness with me; for it is there that you will be aware, at last, of the true reality."

The Priest took me to a garden that is not far from here. Although many people have searched for this garden on the physical plane, it can only be found if you are 'in the Spirit.'

The Garden

The beauty of the garden is beyond compare, for it is Eternal Spring there. The lightness, freshness, aliveness and ever-newness that are the essence of the garden were increased because The Priest placed a special helmet on my head as soon as I entered the garden. This was so the light streams of clairvoyance, clairaudience, claircognisance, clairsentinence, clairresonance and clairobservance were enhanced and the clairmonstrance stream was opened out. It enables extrasensory awareness of the level of holiness that has been rendered to all that is in a receptacle such as the Higher Self. In other words, it is so there is a whole sense of The Divine. Once I was used to this stream's higher vibration, I became aware that there was a Mystical Presence in the garden. I knew straightaway that it was Thoth.

The Priest said, "Now that your sense of The Profound had been heightened to this level, you are ready to go with me to Risen Atlantis. I want you to record, and make known the many wonders that you will behold there. Have faith and trust that what will be revealed will not disappoint. By employing the enhanced Gifts of Spirit, things that were concealed and lost to your sight will be viewed through the radiance of the 'Sun' Light and the connection that you will attain with Risen Atlantis will be extraordinarily fruitful."

Risen Atlantis (RA)

As the Gateway to Risen Atlantis opened, The Priest told me that we were going to attend a conference that was being held in the palace of The Temple of The Sun Disc. He explained that the conference was to do with an Alliance between Extraterrestrial Beings and the Human

Race. The Treaty is so our ascension to a higher evolved level of development is not delayed in any way once Risen Atlantis emerges on the physical plane.

The change in humans will be remarkable after the Great Event. We will all be able to tune into higher frequencies and different dimensions and we will be fully aware of the Extraterrestrial Beings who will be living alongside us on Risen Atlantis. The development, in humans, of a finer force is necessary so that what we have achieved so far can be exceeded. Extraterrestrial Beings will be residing on Risen Atlantis with us to establish a secure base so that we can rise to our true greatness.

The Obelisk

The Priest took me to an obelisk first of all as that is where all new arrivals are going to be taken to when they reach the silvery-golden shore of Risen Atlantis.

Etched on the obelisk are the names of all those who have been involved in preparing Atlantis for its re-emergence on the physical plane. As I was looking at the names, I was reminded of the vision that I saw a long time ago of Beings gathered round the mountain of humanity's spiritual inheritance and I remembered their joy at being able to raise it to a higher level.

When I went through the Gateway, Risen Atlantis was shrouded in white mist, but the mist had started to clear now and I saw that the magnificent Temple of The Sun Disc was near to the obelisk.

The Temple of The Sun Disc

We went into the Temple as The Priest was going to consecrate the Holy of Holies. The Temple was filled with beautiful flowers and as their fragrance wafted through the building, I heard a choir singing heavenly harmonies. They were in the Angelic Balcony, which is below God's Balcony and underneath the balconies, in the Holy of Holies, the Holy Vessel, representing the Temple's ethos of pure consciousness, was standing in the loop of a large gold Ankh. All had been made ready.

The Priest went into the Holy of Holies and switched on a powerful force field around the shrine; light from three discs on God's Balcony were directed on to the Ankh; a humming sound, which was coming from deep within the Holy of Holies intensified; the Temple began to shake, and then an explosion of light, which was like a star burst, filled the Holy of Holies. The Almighty One's Name blazed from the Holy Vessel; a whirlwind column of white light rose from the shrine up to God's Balcony, and fiery light started being emitted from the Ankh.

The Priest stretched his arms out along the horizontal bar of the Ankh, kissed the Holy Receptacle, and then bowed as he thanked The Almighty One for the wondrous Light that now filled the Holy of Holies.

The Watchtower

On our way to the palace, The Priest and I stopped at the watchtower. It is also known as 'The Lighthouse' as on the top of the tower there is a large cluster of diamonds. The Priest was going to activate the gemstones so that they produced a covering of high frequency light over Risen Atlantis. I knew that Thoth had instructed The Priest in the art of maximising the power of crystals and gemstones, but I had not been shown how it was done before.

As we climbed up the spiral staircase to the top of the tower The Priest said, "The power that will erupt from these gemstones will be because there is the will within them for it do so, combined with their recognition of my voice. Once it is recognised, I will raise the pitch of my voice to a higher frequency and issue the command 'ACTIVATE.' This will set the power of the light coming from the diamonds at the optimal level."

The Priest began humming and I was aware of the loving kindness that he was transmitting to the diamonds so that the power of the light in the gemstones was gently awakened. He continued communing with the diamonds in this way and gradually the power of the light that was being emitted from the diamonds matched the power of his voice. This indicated that the gemstones were fully attuned to his voice.

The Priest started singing and the frequency on which he pitched his voice caused the diamonds' container to start rotating. Once The Priest commanded the diamonds to activate, the amount of power that was emitted from them was immense. As the high frequency light spread out from the watchtower, it was obvious that the diamonds were operating at their maximum level and now that The Lighthouse was fully operational, The Priest and I set off for the palace.

The Palace

The palace has been built on a hill and it has been coated with the same white substance that was used on the Temple. A special feature of the palace is its domed roof.

The Messenger of the Gods, who became known to the Greeks and Romans as Hermes or Mercury, was waiting inside the palace. We greeted each other warmly and then he took me on a tour of the palace.

The rooms of the palace are spacious, their ceilings are high and they are filled with light. At the back of the palace, on the ground in the garden, there are twelve gold ray-like extensions around a magnificent fountain and it looks as though light is erupting from a huge sun.

I ran into the fountain and joyfully bathed in its sparkling light until The Messenger told me that it was time to go and get ready to attend the conference.

The Conference

Once we were inside the palace, I put on the long white garment that Hermes/Mercury had given me. At Heart Chakra level, on the robe, there was a silvery white star.

The Priest's garment was a lovely shade of electric blue/purple. It was similar in style to my apparel except that there was a white panel down the centre of the robe and many rays of silver light blazed from the star.

On the floor beneath the domed ceiling there is an electric blue circle and in the circle there is a twelve-rayed silver star. The Twelfth Ray pertains to the spiritual attributes that a giant race of Beings will have. When they emerge, they will be mighty in their profound sense of divinity; they will be replete with Divine Wisdom; their hearts will be full of unconditional love, and they will live in peace and harmony with all Beings in the Universe. This is the Divine Plan for the ultimate expression of the Human Race.

Everyone at the conference sat in front of one of the rays of the star. Apart from The Priest, The Messenger and myself, they were the Ascended Master, Serapis Bey; Ezekiel, who is now the Ambassador of Truth for the Inter-Galactic Council; the Master of Ceremonies, Melchizedek, who was the High Priest of old Atlantis; a Giant, three Beings who were called, 'The Wise,' a Delegate called, 'Tesperasperri,'[1] and a female Extraterrestrial Being called, 'Consuael.'[2]

The Messenger told me that this is one of the guises that she adopts; that she is the Mother of The Priest, and reminded me that his Atlantean name was, EAXZOS, which means, *One Called by God to increase Humanity's Attunement to The Light*; that her name means, *Comforter from God*; that Thoth commissioned the Atlantean Sphinx to honour her, and that she would be setting out some of the terms of the Treaty.

---

[1] TESPERASPERRI (tess-per-ass-per-re)
[2] CONSUAEL (con-sway-el)

The Master of Ceremonies stood up and said:-

"The need for immediate action to be taken is ever present. The folly of not being prepared will leave those who are not ready aghast at what will be occurring. There is much that will arise that will seem to be of a calamitous nature. Lights will be seen and there will be much discussion of what they portend. Hopes that have been dashed in those who are ready for the release of more Light in the Universe will rise again. Much work will need to be done to ease the furrowed brows of those who are already struggling to come to terms with the changes that have been taking place in their lives. The release of a flood of knowledge, which has been held in abeyance about the Great Event, will elicit panic in some, disbelief in others and a great sense of relief in those who are prepared for all the changes that are going to occur.

"The diffraction of The Light has been necessary because the best level of understanding that Human Beings were able to muster about The Light fell far short of what was required for a higher level of evolvement to be reached. Progress in this matter is essential. Their DNA is, therefore, being re-configured in a way that would seem alien to them or even to be the result of aliens carrying out experiments on certain members of the Human Race. The time will come when all will be made clear. What will be revealed would not be generally understood at present.

"The next phase of the Divine Plan will be opened out soon. Aside from physical activity, much phenomena of an Extraterrestrial nature will be seen and many will lose their doubts about the existence of Extraterrestrial Beings. It will be realised that they operate on a different frequency to Earth Beings. Some may continue to reject the information that they will be given to begin with, but once the cast of their spiritual eye changes they will no longer be able to deny what is true and as their perception of their neighbours increases, a deeper level of resonance will be attained with them and eventually they will accept the love of their neighbours."

Melchizedek sat down and the Trinity of 'The Wise' stood up. As they began speaking, the vast field of their consciousness opened out and they were surrounded by white light. They spoke these words in a very loving way:-

"We greet those whose past lives have made them realize that Heaven is on Earth in this paradise. We were very sad about the demise of the first Atlantean paradise and overjoyed when we heard that Atlantis was going to rise.

"With tenderness, love and care, for those who will be joining us here, we are building a bountiful path so that all can rise.

"The bridge that is being erected is so the rejected, the resurrected and even those who have been elected can cross over together to a more profound level of being and rise.

"Risen Atlantis will be a glorious sight to all who have been waiting a long time to be granted the right to dwell here in peace and harmony with The Light as they rise.

"A beam of light will come down; the place will be marked where Atlantis will rise, and all here will be able to see the Face of the One Who is going to bestow grace upon the whole Universe by creating a New Dawn of The Light of the World as the Atlantean Sun starts to rise.

"We lift up our hearts and we lift up our eyes, to the One whose wisdom is far greater than all the wisdom possessed by all who are wise, as we make Atlantis ready so that all can rise."

It was the turn of the Delegate who was a giant next. His appearance was humanoid and his thick dark hair was cut in a modern earthly style. As he started talking, I detected a gentle lilt in his voice. His contribution to the conference was as follows:-

"Ground has been gained along with the land that has been reclaimed and preparations are moving ahead quickly for Atlantis to rise.

"Risen Atlantis will be a fine place to live due to what is being achieved by those who have been keeping the faith; fully releasing past associations, and maintaining good relationships with all those who are involved with the emergence."

The Delegate called, Tesperasperri, gave his report sitting down. He was wearing something on his face that looked like a transparent elephant's trunk. I realised that it was some kind of breathing device to demonstrate the problems being caused by the pollution that has occurred to the oceans and waterways of Earth. He gave a detailed explanation of the destruction that Human Beings are causing to the land as well.

The last speaker was Consuael. She was wearing a silver catsuit and a special headdress that looked something like a circuit board. I realized that the headdress was a symbol of the holiness of her connection to The Light. It consisted of small sparkling diamonds and as she spoke different parts of the 'board' lit up. She said:-

"Dear Ones, we are here to form an Alliance with Earth Beings that will be of benefit to them and us. The time has come for them to be fully aware of our presence. There cannot be any further delay as the Great Event is almost upon Earth Beings. We can help them adapt to the changes that will be taking place; but their co-operation will need to be of the highest order. Peace be with you, Earth Beings, we come in peace."

Consuael proposed that time was set aside on another occasion to go more fully into the benefits of the Alliance. She proceeded to give a brief outline of the terms of the Treaty as follows:-

1. The advice that will be given on how to uphold the sanctity of The Treaty will be adhered to rigorously.

2. The breaching of any of the terms of The Treaty by either side will cause the forfeiting of certain privileges that will have been gained due to the level of co-operation that will have been opened out by either side.

3. Extraterrestrial Beings have been given a voice so that they can share the knowledge that they have about the true meaning of Life on Earth and also so they can seed a new level of understanding, in humankind, of The Light. The messages will be clear so that misunderstandings will not be able to arise.

4. One of the benefits of The Alliance will be the sharing of information, with Earth Beings, about wormholes as it will enable travel between dimensions to become commonplace for them. An era of increased prosperity and well being for those on Earth will be the result.

Light started being emitted from Consuael's headdress and she was able to directly project images into everyone's field of vision. First of all, Consuael showed us the two wormholes through which entry to her underwater base is attained. Then we were guided to a large hanger, at the base, in which there was a silver cigar shaped vehicle. Next, we were able to experience what it was like to travel in the craft and go through Light Zones that Human Beings, in general, are not aware of because they are not attuned to their higher frequencies.

After the presentation, we were treated to an exquisite performance of the symphony called, 'Risen Atlantis.' As the symphony's higher harmonies filled the room, the domed ceiling above us opened and a beam from The Light of SHI entered the chamber. It illuminated the face of one of the Delegates and in a flash, the site where Atlantis will re-emerge on the physical plane was revealed. Everyone in the room then received a personal message from The Source of All Wisdom and mine was as follows:-

"Dear One, I light your mind with Soul Wisdom. I caress your heart with My Deep Love. I make you aware of My Presence in myriad ways. My Presence is like a star that has yet to be appreciated in all its glory. My features can be discerned, but a veil still covers their true appearance. A feature that you have lost sight of will be redeemed once a special journey has been made. As you have been singing, with all your heart, about wanting to attain a higher level of harmony with the Robe of My Light, the Violet Robe will descend upon you and you will be able to see the White Flame in all its glory."

The Ascension Chamber

The Ascended Master, Serapis Bey, is the Keeper of the White Flame and once I was attired in the Violet Robe, he came forward and took me to his Ascension Chamber on Risen Atlantis.

I had met Serapis Bey before in Atlantis and Egypt and I had visited his Atlantean Crystal City when I was an Acolyte. He was just the same as I remembered him. It always felt as though my whole being was smiling when I was in his presence due to his huge personality and jovial manner.

Serapis Bey's Ascension Chamber on Risen Atlantis is deep inside the base of a cliff. Access is gained to the room through a tunnel on the right side of the cliff. First, we entered a huge chamber called the Map Room. In the centre of the Map Room there is an enormous table. Many maps and charts of all kinds were strewn across the table and beside it I saw something that looked like a periscope. It went through the ceiling of the Map Room. The chamber is circular and there is a bookcase next to each of its arches. Access is gained to other parts of the cliff complex through these arches.

The White Flame

The arch that leads to the Ascension Chamber is directly in line with the table in the Map Room and as we approached the chamber I could see the White Flame. The power of its light took my breath away and I realised that the Violet Robe was not only to protect me, but also to raise my vibration so that I could enter the room that contained the White Flame.

The Ascension Chamber is also circular and archways lead from it to other rooms, but it is different from the Map Room in that the walls are covered with mirrors so that there are many images of the White Flame in the chamber and the Flame can be seen from different angles depending on where you are standing in the room. The Flame seems to emerge from a hole in the ground.

As I gazed at the beauty of the White Flame and absorbed its purity, I felt a very strong surge of energy rise up my central light column and I saw that my subtle column was filled with pure white light. My Heart Chakra opened and I received the following message:-

The force in the Divine Spark has been intensified otherwise the knowledge that is going to be revealed to you would be too great for you to assimilate. The surge of Heavenly Energy will enable much that has been hidden to be revealed to you. You are ready to accept the challenge to attain a greater level of understanding of My Light. Persevere, Dear One, and you will be amazed at what will be opened out to you.

The light of the flame became even brighter and I realized that an immense amount of power was being directed into the Flame as it suddenly rose up and went through the ceiling of the chamber. Serapis Bey told me that the Flame is the force that is driving the re-emergence of Atlantis on the physical plane and that what I had just witnessed was a significant part of the preparations that are taking place for this to occur. The Ascended Master then took me into the chamber that is behind the Flame.

The Crystal Chamber

On a stand in the centre of the chamber there is a huge white quartz crystal. I had been able to put my hands on this stone when I visited Serapis Bey's Atlantean Crystal City, but a grid of white tendrils of massive electrical power has formed round the crystal now and I grasped that the connection between the Flame and the crystal was of the utmost importance.

In an alcove on the right side of the large white crystal there is a gold Ankh and on the wall opposite it there is an enormous gong. Serapis Bey informed me that when the gong is struck, it will signify that the New Dawn of The Light in the World has been brought into being.

Before I began the special journey that I had been told that I would undertake, the Ascended Master gave me a piece of the white quartz crystal. It had been fashioned so that it represented the cosmic egg which according to some, had been formed when the first sound emerged. The cosmic egg is associated with a great transformation taking place and etched on the front of the crystal egg that Serapis Bey gave me there is a multi-rayed Star.

After I had thanked the Ascended Master for the gift of the crystal, he took me through an archway on the left side of the Ascension Chamber that led to a white spiral staircase. As I ascended, via the staircase to the top of the cliff, my heart was singing the higher harmonies that I had heard being sung in The Temple of The Sun Disc, by the Angels in the Atlantean Choir; for to learn more about The Light is my heart's greatest desire.

THE WITNESS

PART II

The Special Message

DON'T LET THE STORM CLOUDS WORRY YOU

*You are working with your
highest spiritual energy.
Stay positive.
All is well.*

MARION LAWRENCE

The Angel of Atlantis called, EZMERRYAEL,[1] was waiting for me on the cliff top. EESH[2] enormous wings were furled and as I gazed at the Angel, an image of a swan came to mind. I was entranced by the purity of the light that surrounded EZMERRYAEL and the words, "The Angel of The Lord came down and glory shone around" resonated in my heart.

Behind us there was a large pyramid. The gold light that was being emitted from the building caused it to look as though it was made of glass. The symbol of Risen Atlantis, which I had seen in a temple in Egypt a long time ago, of the Benu/Phoenix bird, had been positioned above the entrance. Its wings were raised indicating that it was about to rise from its three legged perch of past, present and future.

---

[1] EZMERRYAEL (ez (as in fez)-mer (rhymes with fur)-rye-ay (as in hay)-el (as in fell)

[2] EESH (e (as in fee)-eshhh (as in mesh) – (This word is the personal pronoun for an Angel as Angels are genderless.)

Above the Risen Atlantis symbol, I could see the white crystalline equidistant cross, which is the Holy Symbol of The Source of All Wisdom. The light coming from the cross indicated that it was being projected, from inside the pyramid, on a very high frequency. My attention was then drawn to The Priest. He was standing next to the entrance to the pyramid and as he stared straight ahead, the expression on his face made me turn round.

The Intruder

On the horizon there was a menacing dark cloud and I felt afraid of what it might mean. EZMERRYAEL said, "Fear not, for all will be well," and wrapped EESH downy soft white cloak of invisibility around me.

The Angel pointed out that further along the cliff top the top part of the 'periscope,' which I had seen in the Map Room, was trained on a black vehicle that was something like a helicopter.

The craft landed in front of the pyramid and the being that emerged from the vehicle made me gasp with horror as he had been one of the Sons of Belial. In other words, his evil ways had contributed to the destruction of old Atlantis.

He was wearing armour, but it was not bright and shiny. It was dark and damaged reflecting his true nature. Over the top of his armour he wore a black cape and on his chin he wore a false beard that was similar to the ones that pharaohs in Egypt wore. A tuft of black hair had been attached to the bottom of the beard.

Although the intruder had not seen me, I realized that he had seen the white cross on the front of the pyramid. It was obvious that it had spooked him because he hastily got back into the vehicle. As it took off, a white flame was emitted from the 'periscope' and the craft and its occupant were vaporized.

The last thought that I had had before old Atlantis disappeared beneath the waves was that the Temple Vessel must not fall into the wrong hands. This fear had obviously stayed with me. All the time that I had been on Risen Atlantis, I had been concerned that the Sons of Belial would return, when Atlantis re-emerged on the physical plane, and start misusing the advanced technological knowledge that the inhabitants are going to receive from the Extraterrestrial Beings. The Angel hugged me very lovingly and said, "Peace be with you, Dear One of Soul Sight. This past association had to be fully released before more information could be opened out to you about the White Flame, its power and its protection of Risen Atlantis."

The Golden Pyramid of Risen Atlantis

EZMERRYAEL told me that I could now go into the pyramid and that Serapis Bey was waiting for me there. As I entered the building I noticed, at once, that it had been built directly above the Ascension Chamber as the White Flame rose up the centre of the pyramid and went through the place where the capstone would normally be situated. I could now see that the core of the flame was a spiral and as I watched its continuous upward motion, I was aware of my vibration being raised again and intense joy flooded into my Heart Chakra.

The Crystal Booth

On the right side of the pyramid behind the White Flame there is a booth. When I went into it, I saw that the booth contains many quartz crystals. I was surprised to hear sounds coming through the crystals, but the mystery was solved as soon as I realised that an aerial came down through the pyramid into the booth.

I held the cosmic egg crystal that Serapis Bey had given me against my Heart Chakra and I was able to receive the message that was being broadcast by the Inter-Galactic Council that I was to make known when I returned to the physical plane:-

"Earth Beings, forsake unnecessary outer exploration of your galaxy. Go within and accumulate knowledge so that a higher level of understanding is gained about The Light."

Serapis Bey then took me up a flight of stairs, at the back of the pyramid, that led to the roof top.

The Cosmic Cloud Craft

As I went out on to the roof top, I saw that above the White Flame there was an extremely bright multi-rayed Star from which Holy Light was pouring. The message that I received from The Source of All Wisdom was as follows:-

"Dear Beloved One, you have managed to redeem a feature that you lost sight of long ago. It has appeared in this form because it was the level of understanding of Me that you had at that time. You will now be able to go beyond this emanation so that you can attain the fullest level of understanding of My Light that you can tolerate at this time."

A long white cloud suddenly appeared and docked next to the pyramid. The Being who emerged from the vehicle had a bald normal size human head, but a longer neck. His head and neck were surrounded by gold light.

The Being helped me gain entry to the Cosmic Cloud Craft and the first thing that I noticed about it was that the far end of the vehicle consisted of a large circle of gold light that looked like the sun that we see on Earth.

The 'sleeping' quarters were positioned on the side of the craft and at the front of the vehicle there were many screens and a large control panel. Each of the buttons on the panel made a sound and for their functions to be fully operational, all the sounds had to be in harmony with each other.

There was a large button in the centre of the control panel which made a discordant sound. It activated a shield so that the craft was undetectable. I was made aware that the intricacy of the design of the craft far exceeded anything that Human Beings could dream of designing at present to explore our own galaxy. As a consequence, I felt very honoured to have been granted permission to enter this vehicle.

The Special Journey

The gold circle started rotating, the craft began moving, and 'in the blink of an eye' it had reached a dimension that was above the one on which I had been viewing Risen Atlantis.

The level of the dimension that I was taken to was cloaked in white light. In the centre of this light I saw what looked like a white lotus flower that had numerous petals, except that its many petals were in fact flames.

As I gazed at the flames, I was aware of the level of holiness that this vision encapsulated as I was able to see the silver Spark that was at the centre of the 'flower.' Each sparkling, dancing light coming from the Spark made a connection with the divine spark in my being.

I could hear a continuous clicking sound and recognised it as being one of the vibrations that constituted The Name of SHI. I realized that it was related to my attunement to The Light of SHI being raised. When the highest frequency on which I could tolerate The Light was reached, the clicking sound stopped and was replaced by the sound of the Breeze of the Holy Spirit wrapping round me.

Now that The Light of SHI had been opened out on a frequency that I had not been able to experience before, my awareness of the depth of highest love became so intense that I thought that it was going to be more than I could bear, and then a profound feeling of peace engulfed me. After awhile, I felt a tingling sensation in the area of my Crown Chakra and I received the following message:-

"Dear One of Soul Sight, you have been able to access a level that was beyond your vision before and you are now ready to assimilate the information that you are going to be given.

"A baby will be born who will possess a vast level of Divine Power. The haze that will surround the identity of the baby will be removed to coincide with the Light phenomena that will herald the start of the Great Event. You will recognise the baby's Atlantean features. Her face will be beautiful in a way that has not been seen for a long time. A feature that will particularly stand out will be a star shaped birthmark on her forehead. There will not be any doubt about the divine nature of the child's birth as it will be realized that she is one in whom a higher level of evolvement has been awakened. Her level of intelligence will be a revelation; her level of insight will be revolutionary, and the level of holiness that will be in her will be instantly recognised. This is because the light that will surround the baby will generate understanding of her profound resonance with Me. The child will develop at a phenomenal rate and will be ready to take on the role that she came to Earth for within a few years of reaching the current age for attendance at school because the power of Absolute Love will grow in her exponentially. The name of this shining Being of Light will be, LLLAEL,[1] which means, 'the Peace of God.' The New Dawn of The Light in the World will be a welcome sight to those who have been waiting for Atlantis to rise."

I sat in deep contemplation of this information for some time until, with a jolt, I realized that the Cosmic Cloud Craft had arrived back at the pyramid and that it was time for me to disembark. After I had thanked the Being who had taken me on such a very special journey, I saw that Serapis Bey had been waiting for me on top of the pyramid. The Ascended Master drew my attention to a massive mountain of white light that extends high above the whole of Risen Atlantis. It is there to protect the island and its inhabitants.

[1] LLLAEL (l-l-l-ay-el (as in fell)

The Ceremony

As soon as I had joyfully told the Ascended Master all about my special journey, he said that a Ceremony was about to begin, outside the pyramid, during which Risen Atlantis was going to be blessed.

All the Beings, who had gathered on the cliff top next to the pyramid, were involved with the preparations for Atlantis to rise and led by Melchizedek, they sang this blessing, accompanied by the Atlantean Angelic Choir:-

"May Risen Atlantis be a place of Peace, Deep Divine Peace,
Deep Divine Peace, forevermore.
May Risen Atlantis be a place of Joy, Deep Divine Joy,
Deep Divine Joy, forevermore.
May Risen Atlantis be a place of Love, Deep Divine Love,
Deep Divine Love, forevermore.
May Risen Atlantis be a Beacon of Light, a beautiful
Beacon of Light, forevermore.

Melchizedek then placed a large silver brick on the right side of the pyramid. This brick is the cornerstone for the Library that is going to be erected there. The Library that the Atlanteans established in Alexandria, Egypt, was so highly regarded that it is still talked about even though it was destroyed a long time ago. The new Library will be built first and then a University will be constructed on the left side of the pyramid. Silver symbolises the Higher Wisdom that is going to be gained due to the ascension of consciousness of The Almighty One, Who is The Source of All Wisdom, All Light, All Energy, Absolute Love and All That Is.

A tower is going to be put up in a courtyard in the centre of the Library's buildings. The material used to construct the tower will contain a metallic like substance called, 'orchialcum,' which "sparkles like fire." The 'fire' reflects the beautiful otherworldly hues of pinks and reds, orange and yellows, and silvery rose gold as these are the colours that are seen as the Atlantean Sun rises. The Atlantean Flag will be placed on top of the tower. The tower will be very tall so that it can be seen from afar. The height will signify the height of learnedness that will be able to be attained from studying the treasured manuscripts and esoteric works etc. that will not be available anywhere else. As a place of research, it will not be equalled. Beings from other dimensions, as well as humankind from all the nations of Earth, will travel to Atlantis to gain admittance to the Library. The building of such a prestigious Library was included in the Divine Plan for the resurrection of Atlantis as it is going to be 'a many splendoured' place of higher evolvement.

The Location of Risen Atlantis

For centuries, Atlantis has been partially rising to the surface before disappearing again beneath the waves of consciousness; but now that a portal has been opened, the tide will go out completely. "There will be no more sea,"[1] just an Ocean of Light.

One of the speakers at the conference that I attended in the palace was a giant. His Irish name is 'Fionn mac Cumhaill,'[2] and he is associated with the Giant's Causeway in Northern Ireland. The significance of him attending the conference is that the portal has been opened in that area of the United Kingdom and at present, Risen Atlantis is in the Intertidal Zone of Spirit that is there.

When the Great Soul of Light Supreme appears, the veil will be removed; the unseen will become visible, and Atlantis will emerge. The Atlantean Flag will be unfurled heralding the start of the New Dawn of The Light in the World and in accordance with God's Grace, the Atlantean Race will rise again albeit in a different place and a different time; for God's Time will reign on the Earthly Plane.

---

[1] Revelation 21:1
[2] Fionn mac Cumhaill (Finn macCool)

THE MESSENGER

TRANSFORMATION

*Transformation will be to a more
spiritual way of thinking and living,
from the blossoming of Spiritual Gifts.*

MARION LAWRENCE

My spiritual odyssey and the long journey that other Atlanteans have undertaken will soon be at an end. It has certainly been eventful. The dispersion of the Atlantean Race led to many of us experiencing lifetimes in a variety of locations around the World; but now the long awaited homecoming is in sight.

The culmination of my odyssey is to make known the following messages. On many occasions, I have felt overwhelmed by the responsibility that comes with carrying and then, at the pre-ordained time, delivering messages of this nature. I am grateful that the training that I undertook very many moons ago provided all messengers of The Order of Human Messengers of The Divine with this advice:-

"Let the knowledge that is in your heart flow unhindered, and trust that The Light will direct it to the places that it needs to go to. The success of the mission will be measured by the hope that the positive perspective brings."

The messages are profound. They are to awaken those who are still asleep and in the dark about the Great Event, and to bring joy to those who are already awake in The Light. Illuminating and inspiring, they convey how the changes that will be taking place are in accordance with The Source of All Wisdom's Grace.

≡<>≡

The New Dawn of The Light in the World

"A standing feature of Earth is its durability. It is able to withstand many changes, disruptions and upheavals. There are more to come. Significant happenings will take place leading up to the Great Event. The aura around the moon will be extended; the sun's ejections will increase; new constellations will become visible. Significant happenings are occurring to Human Beings too, but they are being alerted to the fact that there is the potential for a great disaster to occur to this Civilisation.

"The Fate that awaits humankind is unavoidable unless a change of direction is made. A catastrophic experiment that took place a long time ago, when there was a decline in spiritual development, was on a scale that nearly caused the annihilation of all that had been created to live on Earth. This is a reminder that there are forces that are far more powerful than can be understood in human terms. It is evidence of the consequences of ceasing to abide by the law that governs these forces. Willingness to learn from the past is the key to everything not having to begin again."

The Fall

"The Fall contributed to the passage of time being inhabited by humankind. It is thought by some that the total tariff of The Fall is being paid for in instalments, and that there will never be a time when Human Beings will be released from the debt.

"Others have predicted that "fire, brimstones, doubt and ladles of the soup of cast off woes" will all come before the day when the Great Light shines down on the people. For those desperately seeking solace, suspend all beliefs that humankind are being punished for past sins. The following information is being presented to Human Beings so that they realize that something that many consider to be of value should be relinquished as it is contributing to the chaos that exists on the physical plane.

"The proposal that led to The Fall was that when there were enough free thinkers The Will of The Divine would be accommodated again. Instead, humankind has continued to act as though they have 'free will,' and so they are ruled by Fate. Abandoning the system of thought that belongs to the lower planes of consciousness will bring about the demise of Fate. To compensate for the so called loss of 'free will,' Gifts of Spirit will be activated in Human Beings that they could not gain access to before. When they reach the level of peace that harmonises with the peace of the Great Soul of Light Supreme, the spiritual wealth that will be given to humankind, by The Divine, will elicit awe and true humility.

"It will take time, for some Human Beings, to assimilate what humanity's escape from the clutches of Fate will mean. Resounding success is not predicted until after the Great Event when the eagerness of humanity to change its understanding will be very apparent. Earth Beings will realise the necessity for reformation and haste will occur in re-assembling the substance of human life to fit the new framework that they will be given.

Preparations for The Great Event

"The flow of Light in the Material World is being increased to illuminate issues that are holding back the spiritual development of the Race, which is also being hampered by those who are keeping it constrained within boundaries that are limiting its growth. Widespread disillusion with the diocesan is having an effect. The diocesan collections have been greatly reduced highlighting the lessening of the Church's authority. Distrust mixed with a glimmer of hope will be replaced with full faith when the Parish Church and the Brethren are superseded by the Cathedral of Light, and there is total parity of the sexes. The habit will be replaced with a flowing gown of white light, and women will bring forth the missing links that will enable a greater level of understanding of religious thought. Bias has formed for one method of instruction over another. Each holds details that are relevant; but when the Great Light appears they will be cast off as one path will be followed and direct experience of The Divine will be attained by all.

"A large amount of authority has been handed over to rulers and governments too. The influence of those who are corrupt is causing widespread damage to be caused to Earth. The pursuance of the riches of the land has almost wiped out its resources in some areas of the World; poisoning its soil is bringing more disease as it is becoming devoid of nutrients; deforestation has led to a burden being placed on other resources; people have been left distraught at the demolition of the habitat of animals leading to their extinction, and pollution of the waterways is contributing to the possibility that humankind's life on Earth will not continue indefinitely. Destroying the ecology is madness. Earth will become a barren wilderness if ways are not found to halt the destruction. Instead of taking from it all the time, something needs to be given back to Earth. A resolution to abide in peace with Earth must be made. Nurture Earth and then it will continue to nurture you.

"From parchment to paper, progression continues as ideas take form. Existing formulations are fragmenting to make way for the new. The fleeting system is ready for replacement. Understanding that the system in its present form cannot carry on for much longer will abound. It will lead to desperate measures being taken. Oppressed by the deceit of those who do not believe in transparency, people are starting to rebel against the rulers who have kept them in poverty financially and spiritually. The dissonance will reach a crescendo and it will culminate in the rising of the distressed and the diseased.

"It is believed by some Human Beings, who are struggling with the intransigence of the minority that are intent on causing destruction and disharmony, that devoid of the presence of mind to save their souls from destruction, those powered by the forces of evil will discover the price of their darkness soon. References have been made to Armageddon. The worst scenario has been contemplated by them and they maintain that the precedent for 'free will' was set so that intervention was ruled out until bombardment reached a level where human existence could not be sustained; that the wreaking of such carnage would clear the way for a new beginning, and that when the Great Battle erupts there will not be any dispute about what people are dying for as those who die in service to The Light will be resurrected wholly as Light Beings.

"A tally has been kept of the minor sorties by a growing number of people. They have realised the futility of wars and have come to the conclusion that armaments designed to halt the flow of aggression have exacerbated the problem. They believe that there is a better way than the one that is being followed at present and that a calamity will not arise because humankind will draw back from the brink just in time and summon The Army of The Light. The vibrations through which prayers are received are listened to attentively. The Army of The Light surround the Material World. They were sent by The Source of All Wisdom so that as soon as Human Beings ask, they can be given all the help that they need.

"The Army of The Light gave assurances a long time ago that they would return and they will arrive at the twelfth hour to make sure that all goes well at the Great Event. The Alliance means that they are going to help humankind prepare for the next stage of their evolution so that the right path is taken – the one that leads to the betterment of all, not just Earth Beings, as humanity is holding back the ascension of others in the Universe. The Source of All Wisdom loves all those in the Universe to such an extent, and so deeply, that *Yish*[1] is raising the light frequency to a higher level than it has vibrated on during this Civilisation's occupancy of Earth. Evolution is the key: progress is essential. The Almighty One has decreed that the entire Human Race must ascend. There cannot be any dissenters. The forsaking of the lower planes of consciousness is for the pursuit of the goal of an advanced level of development. It can only be attained by vacating the lower planes.

"The Army of The Light has appointed Messengers to assure humankind that the ascension that will be undertaken will bring many benefits; to set their minds at rest that peace will be the outcome, and to make them aware of how much they are cherished. Members of The Order of Human Messengers of The Divine and The Army of The Light are bearers of the Holy Symbol and once there is acceptance that The Army of The Light is an Extraterrestrial Force and that they are in service to The Almighty One, much that has been a mystery will fall into place.

"Messengers are coming from all over the physical world to share the wisdom that they have been given. Each day brings forth new avenues of awareness, lighting pathways with streams of higher consciousness as never before. Light Workers are engaged in many different projects. The passing of time has left the majority of the Human Race unsure of the true nature of members of The Army of Light Beings. To diminish the fear that may arise in Human Beings at the thought of the Material World being taken over by a Great Force, Messengers will continue to bring uplifting news to help them get through the remaining days of darkness before the Great Light appears. Eventually, understanding will be gained that the changes were necessary so that the ascension of the consciousness of the Human Race to a higher evolved level could take place.

[1] *Yish* (eye-ee-shhh). This word is the personal pronoun for The Almighty One Who is beyond gender.

"The variety of social structures will continue for awhile. If a sign is required that all is being made ready for the Great Event, the way the darkness in the 'shadow side' of humanity is being exposed is proof. Much that is not of The Light is being swept away in what appears to be a very short time. Scandal after scandal has erupted; people are being brought to justice for crimes that they committed years ago, and the impeachments that have occurred are further evidence of the changes that are taking place. Government Ministers, Police Officers, Bankers and Priests are no longer exempt as the full extent of the mastery of those with the disposition to deceive is being exposed. Those who think that their power and wealth makes them invincible are discovering that the exploitation of the vulnerable will not be tolerated. The World is awry because of the divide between nations' wealth and although charitable works have been carried out in poorer countries, much more needs to be done to alleviate the suffering caused by those who ruthlessly set about destroying any opposition to the power of corrupt governments and establishments. The eventual breakdown of the way that they are run will lead to the development of all nations. The ablutions will continue to take place to ensure that Earth Beings are ready for the Great Event.

"Many years have passed as The Army of The Light waited for this time to be fulfilled. It is especially poignant for these Beings as they want this Civilisation to succeed. When the Extraterrestrial Beings appeared on Earth before, it heralded the start of an upward step in the evolution of humankind. Small amounts of extra knowledge were given, with great love, about the Great Event. Many souls, and many more of every kind, have carried forward the knowledge that a Heavenly Being placed in their hearts' energy centre a long time ago and now these valuable keepsakes are going to be activated. Their use is sacred; they hold great power. What was lost will be revealed again and mysteries that have clothed the collective human consciousness for so long will be removed. The constancy with which the passing over of knowledge will be taking place after the

Great Event is a sign of The Will of The Divine for the World to be a better place. Human Beings are not ready for this influx of knowledge yet.

"The asunder of the existing condition and the re-arrangement of the human soul's energy force for the finer, higher frequency is accented in humans who have already attained the faculties that the Higher Self possesses. Enmeshed in the Light Body is a deep level of awareness of The Light. It has not been possible for most people to access it, but the powers that have been given to some mean that they are attuned to The Light to a greater extent than is normal. It has enabled understanding of the higher harmonies of the Divine Plan for humankind to be gained. This gift is bestowed according to the Grace of The Source of All Wisdom. The reason that these souls attained this level of enlightenment is due to the sacrifices which many of them made, in previous lives, so that there could be the attainment, by all, of a higher evolved level of consciousness. *Yish* Mercy was brought forth as a result and much help will be given to assist the continuation of Project Earth."

The Great Event

"After the tumultuous years preceding the Great Event, the mass of humanity will be migrating to a Higher Dimension. The alignment of the Forces to bring about the Great Event will be beyond the current understanding of humankind. The power of The Light that is in all that has been manifested by All That Is, is being enhanced for a New Dawn of The Light in the World. The Almighty One has decreed, and so it will be brought into manifestation. The Light will prevail. Details will be given of how events will fall into place in the order of things divine.

"The profound nature of what will occur will mean that all that seems to be real will be realized to be unreal because of an adjustment of focus. For too long the focus of the majority of Human Beings has been on the physical world resulting in them being unaware of their true nature. Beset by problems of a seemingly unsolvable nature, a dramatic course of action will follow. What has been in abeyance will be brought forward. The time is near when The Light will burst through into human consciousness. The change that will take place will highlight the haphazard nature that previously existed of understanding about The Light. Instead of each lifetime being an opportunity for an expansion of consciousness of the Earthly Realm, higher and higher levels of consciousness of the Heavenly Realms will be attained. Extraterrestrial Beings will assist this process.

"A mighty undertaking has been given that a trail of flaming, vibrant light will engulf Earth Beings. Humanity will be separated from what it has been given so it can attain the highest components that it is possible for humankind to receive from the Higher Causal Planes. The surrender of human thought to highest thought is a vital part of the intricate mechanism of the Heavenly Plan. Giving back to The Source of All Wisdom what has been given is the revelation of a truth of great magnitude. Something from the very highest level is going to be coming through to the earthly consciousness, which is being heightened to facilitate understanding of the Peace of God. The greatness of the Power of The Light will be visible for all to see.

"The start of the auspicious action will be recognised without doubt. The fleet of heavenly vehicles that will be seen arriving will be as a result of a distress call from those on Earth. The sky will be filled with strange craft. The shock of this will be experienced worldwide. The time is nearly upon Human Beings when they will learn that they are definitely not alone in the Universe.

"A chariot of fire from Heaven will be burning brightly for days so that its significance cannot be missed. Shining Beings of Light will emerge from the vehicle. Understanding of their appearance will be opened out in Human Beings once they have attained a higher level of harmony with the Heavenly Beings as the Illustrious Ones will have arrived to show humankind how they can progress from their present state of chaos. They will seek out special places that are already known to those who have ceased to register the narrow divide between all forms and have joined with The Army of The Light to celebrate, with joy, the Oneness that will occur.

"When the Great Day starts, a buzzing sound will be heard. It will signify that the powerful upgrading of the frequency will have begun. The sound will not affect those who are prepared. They will know to go within and take note of the inner signs. This will help them to withstand the pressure of the outer chaos. Information about the various actions that will need to be taken will be placed in their willing hearts. Heavenly assurances are given that all will be safe when the precipitous event takes place.

"The magnificent glory, magnificent power of The Light of The Almighty One will be revealed to an extent that has not been experienced before. Its radiance will outshine any light that has been manifested. Solar light gives an indication of the brightness of The Light. The fiery Light will penetrate the dense energy of the physical plane and the effect will be something like an x-ray. Objects will fade slightly in intensity and their atomic structure will be able to be seen. Matter will not be the same as it was before. The Light Bodies of Earthly Beings will be revealed. Darkness, in the form of ignorance, will fall away as the denser layers are removed and will be replaced with light, in the form of knowledge. Shadows will be shadows no longer. The finer vibration of the Ultimate Human Being will be portrayed and the Light Bodies of Beings who function on different frequencies to humankind will be able to be seen from then on in accordance with the Great Shift.

"The Light will be seen in Rotorunga, New Zealand; Western Australia; and Minnesota, North America, first. Around the ninth hour, the frequency will change. A momentary pause will take place. The buzzing sound will cease. There will be complete silence. Then the Voice of The Almighty One, which is similar to the sound of thunder, will be heard by every Human Being; for these words will reverberate deep within them:-

"Soul of Light,
AWAKEN.
"Remember the Words of Light; rejoice in the raising of the veil that has covered the memory of them. They are your heritage. You come from The Light. Remember now how your being is made of light. A new light will shine on all aspects of earthly life. The sound of My Voice will resonate in your Heart Chakra with utter clarity. There will be no doubt about its power. To try and continue to ignore My Voice will be futile. There is nothing to fear. My Love will comfort you; My Love will heal all that has gone before; My Love will guide you in the ways of the state of higher evolved consciousness."

"For the total surrender of human thought to highest thought, what was prophesied will take place - The Source of All Wisdom will have spoken to all incarnate beings and those who are still in the dark will finally awaken from the dream of human existence. When the Great Light shines down on them they will realize that chaos and calamity ensues when there is separation from The Light and the pathway will be seen that leads to a better life. Once the spiritual eye is fully opened, the conveyance of an abundance of inner images is commensurate with the peace that is in the heart. A human soul arrives at peace by connecting to The Light. When Human Beings reach out to The Source of All Wisdom, peace will arrive on the wings of love and a bridge of rainbow light will carry them over to a higher level of existence.

"The release of the pressure that will have built up in those who had not accepted that a great change to their existence would be occurring will enable a range of mounting advancements to be put into place. The retrieval of all that has been lost in the ensuing years since the last field of exemplary particles was activated will result in a wealth of knowledge being obtained by the Human Race about the World of Light. An upgrading of the Human Being will be brought about so that the next field of exemplary particles can be absorbed. Once this has taken place, the abiding force will be transformed for the new level of existence.

"The Divine Force within Human Beings will be strengthened so that their realisation of The Source of All Wisdom is at a higher level. The light that will flood in to the Heart Chakras of all will be blessed with the Holy Essence of The Source of All Wisdom. It will bring great richness to the human soul as the hearts of humankind will be filled with love, peace, wisdom, understanding and compassion for all. A meteoric rise in consciousness of I AM will follow. Layer upon layer of Light will have been parted to reach this point of convergence with The Almighty One. There will be rejoicing in the hearts of many and disappointment in the hearts of a few who will think that there is nothing further to discover. They will be wrong, for more will be revealed about The Light than was ever thought possible. Old worn out concepts will be swept away when people are confronted with the Truth; the inclination in the human heart to go to war will cease; violence will come to a standstill, physical weaponry will become obsolete as the ever present fear of destruction will have been removed, peace will spread rapidly, and the level of growth will be phenomenal.

"The nascence will be replete with benefits that had not been available to the majority of people and many good uses will be found for the knowledge that was missing from human endeavours. In each lifetime there will be many more opportunities for growth. Human Beings will no longer be called Homo sapiens instead they will be called MUMU SAPIENS. These Light-words relate to the rebirth of the ultimate expression of the Human Race. Fears such as the intensity of The Light will cause the Human Being to self destruct; the power of the Divine Vehicle will be too great, or the level of perfection will not be able to be maintained will be swept away as soon as it is realized that the ascension will be graded. It will never be more than can be sustained and what will come about will exceed all expectations.

"A Star will appear and its clear shining light will signal the next phase of the Great Event. It will have a royal bearing on what will be opened out. The transition of humankind will be followed by a glorious outcome – they will be re-united with the Great Soul of Light Supreme. There will be a joyous reunion and it will lead to enrichment and certainty; peace and prosperity; ascension and salvation. The New Dawn will bring unprecedented blessings. The powers that are going to be restored to the Human Race are so that its true greatness can be realized. It will truly be an awe inspiring time in the history of humankind."

The New Dawn

"The demise of Fate will enable the level of communion with The Divine that was lost long ago to be resumed. All That Is has decreed that in the New Dawn, there will be understanding of the language that Human Beings have forgotten. The Holy Language of The Light, The Cherishing Language, will resolve many matters of conflict; comprehension will be attained of how the Heavens are configured; certainty about the New World Order will arise in the collective consciousness of humankind, and the Light Words will enable understanding to be attained about time as well.

"The Holy Language of The Light only has one tense; for God's Time is the Eternal Now. When God's Time comes on Earth, The Cherishing Language will be experienced in its true form of flowing light and higher harmonies. There will be nothing to fear by speaking the words; for The Cherishing Language is the outpouring of the warmth of the expression of God's Love for all of Creation. God's Love will be sung in every heart as every Light Word is spoken and the light in human souls will shine through unblemished by their previous animalistic tendencies.

"Disparity will cease and the cast down will be raised. The differences in cultures will meld and ignorance, in the form of racism, will disappear. Order will be restored, and any dissonance will be swiftly forgotten. The clamour to preside over what is to be will be replaced by reverent adherence to The Will of The Divine, and peace will reign.

"Pleasant will be the days of The Alliance. Existence on Earth will be governed by the overwhelming support of each nation to the conglomerate. When the nations are together in this way, matters that arise will be resolved due to The Light shining upon the proceedings. Streams of pure light thought will be received and as a consequence, new avenues of awareness will be brought forth; the advantages of joining with The Army of The Light will be recognized, and bold initiatives will be undertaken.

"Peaceful participation in world affairs will contribute to the nurturing of Earth. Manifold works will be carried out to repair the damage that Human Beings inflicted on the planet, and these endeavours will result in the massive overload on its resources being reduced. The rivers will flow with pure water, the sun will rise and the moon will shine on a world that has changed. Earth will prosper and its bounteous gifts will be shared for the good of all.

"When a milestone has been reached, a discovery will be made that will make way for new treasures to be found. They lie hidden in tunnels and caves, which have kept them safe for thousands of years. A tablet will be discovered that contains the knowledge that is required so that the secrets of these minerals can be unlocked.

"During a summit, which will have been arranged so that the nations can gather together to search for the solution, the codes on the tablet will be deciphered. The worthiness of the human soul distinguishes it from everything else, and deep within it is the higher love for all of Creation. The North will make a pact with the South to deliver the goods once the right way to produce them is understood; the East and West will rise to the challenge to distribute the wealth of the nations evenly.

"The love for The Light that will be in the hearts of all Human Beings will be above all else and it will mean that numerous obstacles will be able to be overcome. Peace and harmony will reign in a glorious episode in this Civilisation's history and great things will be achieved for The Almighty One.

"The long period of peace will demonstrate the advanced state that the Human Race will have reached and that they are ready for the next stage of the Divine Plan to commence; for they have been chosen to generate a New Race. The Divine Vehicle will be used to travel to the galaxy where new life begins and as the Sacred Womb encompasses everything, the Universe will expand within it to accommodate the New Race.

"The birth of the New Race will be attended by many of those who were at the birth of the Human Race. The expertise that the Human Race will have gained through living on Earth, combined with the expansion of their consciousness of The Divine, will be paramount in the rearing of the New Race. From lessons learned concerning the history of the Human Race, a 'fall from Grace' will be avoided. When the New Race 'Comes of Age' and an advanced relationship with The Almighty One manifests, the cycle will begin again."

≡<>≡

Within the messages there is a truth of great worth: sometimes we have to let go of certain things so that something better can take their place. The time is drawing near when the Great Event will begin. Everything is increasing in speed as the slower, denser energy of the Material World is being brought into alignment with the finer, faster energy of the World of Light. By venturing on to the path that you are going to learn about in the next chapter, understanding will eventually be obtained about the whole picture instead of just a part, as knowledge will start to be accessed that Thoth hid in the heart.

MEDITATION

TAKE THE PATH

This path leads you deep inside yourself, connecting you with your inner light, your Teacher.

MARION LAWRENCE

Many benefits await those who persevere with meditation and due to the spiritual development that is achieved, concepts are able to be grasped that may have seemed alien before.

The path that this meditation is going to take you along is the Wisdom Path. The threads of gold light that are sewn through the fabric of all inner life relate to the Wisdom that was bestowed upon you numerous lifetimes ago.

Wisdom is a beautiful energy that has special light and sound qualities that entrance the soul, enliven the soul, expand the soul, and bless the soul. Once access is gained to the Wisdom Path, there is the opportunity for a fortune of immeasurable spiritual wealth to be amassed. The guidelines that follow are to help you to attain the best possible outcome from this meditation:-

First of all, it is important that you turn off your mobile phone and shut the door of the room that you are in so that you will not be disturbed. If possible, sit on a dining room chair. It will help you to keep your back straight so Divine Energy, which is stored in the Base Chakra and is said to uncoil like a snake, can easily rise up your central Light Column to your Third Eye. Keep both of your feet on the floor throughout the whole meditation and make sure that you recite an affirmation, such as the one on P.23, when you start and end the meditation.

<>

Next, place your hands in your lap with your middle fingers touching and your palms against your abdomen. As you breathe in, feel your abdomen expanding and say with your inner voice, *'Energy;'* hold your breath for the count of five, and as you breathe out contract your abdomen as you are saying, with your inner voice, *'Divine Energy.'*

<>

As you breathe in, feel your abdomen expanding and say with your inner voice, *'Harmony;'* hold your breath for the count of five, and as you breathe out contract your abdomen as you are saying, with your inner voice, *'Higher Harmony.'*

<>

As you breathe in, feel your abdomen expanding and say with your inner voice, *'Peace;'* hold your breath for the count of five, and as you breathe out contract your abdomen as you are saying, with your inner voice, *'Deep Peace.'*

<>

Take a deep breath in; turn your hands over so that your palms are facing upwards, with your middle fingers still touching each other, and say, *'Peace,'* with your inner voice, as you slowly raise your hands as high above your head as you are able to reach.

<>

Turn your hands over so that your palms are facing downwards, with your middle fingers still touching each other, and as you breathe out, slowly take your hands back down to your lap while saying, *'Deep Peace,'* with your inner voice. Do the whole exercise two more times with a rhythmic flowing movement.

<>

As Divine Energy rises up your central Light Column, the 'eye of your heart' opens and you see a deep pink flame emerge in your Heart Chakra. A flash of turquoise light appears in your Throat Chakra, indicating that the channel which enables communication with your Teacher has been activated, and then a blaze of intense electric blue light erupts signalling that your Third Eye Chakra has opened.

<>

Now that you have entered a state of Higher Harmony and Deep Peace with Divine Energy, you are able to gain access to the Wisdom Path.

<>

The path takes you straight to a field where there is a stone circle. Stone circles were an important part of the Atlantean tradition of sacred ceremonies and once you enter the field, your attention is drawn to a specific standing stone.

<>

A long time ago the standing stone was engraved with a wisdom teaching ascribed to The Priest of Atlantis, but a chunk is missing from the top left hand corner of the stone.

<>

Fragments from the missing chunk are scattered throughout the field and you feel compelled to go round the field and pick up all the pieces.

<>

When you have found every single one of the fragments and 'glued' them all back together with love, firmly affix the missing chunk to the standing stone so that you are able to read the whole inscription. It says:-

**WHEN THE WELL IS STRUCK,
THE WATER THAT WILL SPRING FORTH
WILL CONTAIN THE BLESSING OF
QUENCHING THE THIRST**

<>

As you are gazing at the words, a connection is made in your Heart Chakra with your Teacher and you receive the following message to help you understand the inscription:-

"Meditation awakens the sleeping Serpent of The Source of All Wisdom and facilitates its uprising from its abode in the Base Chakra. The Serpent then travels up the central light column and strikes the well that is deep within the Heart Chakra so that 'living water'[1] can spring forth. The Serpent continues its journey up to the Third Eye Chakra, which is associated with Christ Consciousness, and heightened awareness of the Mystic Marriage is gained."

<>

Living water, in the form of knowledge, then starts flowing from the well in response to the questions that you ask your Teacher about the Great Event and the New Dawn of The Light in the World.

<>

When your thirst is quenched as fully as possible, at this time, lovingly thank your Teacher; close down the connection by gently putting your earthly mantle back on, and slowly come back to the Material World.

<>

---

[1] "He who believes in Me, as the scripture has said, out of his heart will flow a river of living water." John 7:38

<>

Make sure that you are fully back on the physical plane before you return to your everyday activities. Check that you are grounded by taking your awareness to your feet and consciously feeling beneath them the floor of the room of your dwelling place on the physical plane. Wash your hands and face in cold water and drink a glass of water to complete the grounding process.

<>

The connection that you have made with the Christ Self will enable you to continue along the Wisdom Path more quickly. May your journey be blessed with enlightening experiences and exciting episodes as your attunement to the mystical vibe of Atlantis continues to evolve; and when the time comes for you to beach yourself on its silvery-golden shore, may Risen Atlantis be all that you hoped that it would be and more.

THE HIGHER SELF

HEAVEN IS ON EARTH

*Heaven is on Earth,
if you look through the eyes
of your Higher Self.*

MARION LAWRENCE

The Spiritual Knowledge that Atlanteans possessed was adopted by the Ancient Egyptians and some of their principal teachings were in turn used in early Christianity. In time, the Higher Self also became known as the True Self or Christ Self – the expression of pure consciousness, pure unconditional love.

To live a heavenly life on Earth we need to be like the Higher Self. Adjustments will be made, as a result of the Great Event, so that the attributes of the Higher Self come to the fore.

The reason why our attempts to regain the Atlantean way of life have all failed is because of human nature and so it is being upgraded. The level of refining that will occur will make it impossible for another Fall to take place and when the ultimate expression of the Human Race is brought into being, The Light will shine more intensely in our human selves. It will be a precious time of revival resulting in increased growth.

In order to maintain a heavenly existence, higher and higher levels of consciousness will be able to be reached. Adjustments will continue to be made to the Ultimate

Human Being until it is perfectly attuned to and aligned with the Divine Force and because of the level of resonance that there will be with The Almighty One, all that seemed to be a paradox will be removed. In the meantime, though, how do you tell what is real and what is unreal? You take the Leap of Faith.

Faith is like a lovely flower that grows even more beautiful when it blossoms every day. Its fragrance is exquisite eliciting ever new bliss and as you are meditating, a waterfall of Divine Wisdom will cascade through your awareness; you will be able to view the wonders of Creation that are not seen with the physical eyes, and observe the interconnection of everything – as below so above, as above so below. This will prepare you for when you enter the State of Peace and Harmony, which was known a long time ago as Heaven on Earth; for once you are there, you will be able to inherit all the spiritual wealth that is possessed by the Higher Self.

AS ABOVE SO BELOW

UNIVERSAL WISDOM

*As it is above, so it is below.
As it is below, so it is above.
Above and below are One;
herein lies the key to
all miracles.*[1]

HERMES TRISMEGISTUS

Human consciousness has nearly completed a trek of epic proportions. It has been undertaken in preparation for the monumental journey into Divine Consciousness that our Civilisation will be embarking upon soon. There are, at the very least, several levels on which knowledge about The Divine can be understood and the same applies to Atlantis.

Risen Atlantis is like a mosaic in which all the pieces have been put together to form the complete picture. While we are on the 'film set' of the Outer World at present, though, the 'Kingdom of Heaven' is hidden from physical sight and to some it may seem unreal. When the Third Eye opens during meditation, however, the Mystic Marriage enables insight to be gained concerning Atlantis and the Great Event. That is when the cast of the spiritual eye will be changed. Our perception will then be different of the 'Son,' and in the New Dawn of The Light in the World, we will all be able to view what is above and what is below as One.

---

[1] The Emerald Tablet of Hermes Trismegistus

THANKSGIVING

I AM ALWAYS HERE

In the midst of all confusion,
There is a still Place
Where I am waiting for you,
To heal you, to calm you,
and Love you.
I am always here.

MARION LAWRENCE

In the silence I seek you and from the deep well of peace you rise. Every morning as I greet you, your glorious Light makes me realize how blessed I am to have entered into this Mystic Marriage, for it has opened up my eyes to the unlimited source of ever-new joy, enlightenment, and enrichment that serves to emphasize how sublime direct experience of this Marriage is with you: it is simply divine.

Thank you for making me aware of how much you care. When I breathe out, after I have breathed in and been enveloped by the length and breadth and height and depth of your wondrous love, which is beyond measure, I know full well that this saying is true: "Where your heart is, there you will find your treasure."[1]

---

[1] Matthew 6:21

RECOMMENDED READING

YOUR OWN TRUE NATURE

May your heart remain open;
May you be at peace with
what you discover.
May you awaken to the light
of your own true nature;
May you be healed;
May you be a source of
healing for all beings.

TIBETAN BUDDHIST PRAYER

A Spring Within Us: A Year of Daily Meditations.
Richard Rohr.

'The author draws from Scripture, Christian mystics, non-dual teachers from various faiths and wisdom from other fields such as psychology, science, the Enneagram and Twelve Steps as he encourages us to drink deeply of God's Love.'

The Emerald Tablets of Thoth The Atlantean and The Emerald Tablet of Hermes Trismegistus.
Translated by M. Doreal, Edited by Bart Marshall.

'The Tablet has been described as an extraterrestrial artefact or a gift from Atlantis. It teaches that "All is One" and that direct experience of The Divine is possible through meditation.'

Hymns of Hermes: Ecstatic Songs of Gnosis.
G.R.S. Mead, Introduction by Stephan A. Hoeller.

'Mead draws parallels between Gnostic and Hermetic thought concerning the ecstatic personal experience of The Divine.'

The Gentle Brother: White Eagle's Words to All On The Spiritual Path.
White Eagle Publishing Trust.

'White Eagle's teachings are collected in the form of short extracts to be used as day-to-day readings or to turn to in times of need.'

The Yoga of Jesus.
Self-Realization Fellowship.

'This insightful and compact book transcends the centuries of dogma and misunderstanding that have obscured the original teachings of Jesus, showing that he taught a unifying path by which seekers of all faiths can enter the Kingdom of God.'

> *"If you are serious about learning and studying believe in magic."*
>
> **THOTH, THE ATLANTEAN MASTER TEACHER**
> **(Channelled by Marion Lawrence)**

CONTACT

MAGIC

The second principle of magic: things which have once been in contact with each other continue to act on each other at a distance after the physical contact has been severed.

JAMES G. FRAZER

Dear Cherished Soul Companion,

Thank you for accompanying us to Risen Atlantis. If you want to share with us any impressions that you have gained along the way, we will be very pleased to hear from you. Our contact details are as follows:-

Lindsey: cherishingmeditation@gmail.com

Marion: marionlawrence36@talktalk.net

With Lots of Love
from
Lindsey and Marion

AFTERWORD

GRACE OF THE WAY

This knowledge keep, that it may not dim,
Short arm needs woman and man to reach to Heaven,
So ready is Heaven to stoop to her and him."[1]

FRANCIS THOMPSON

Those who have been waiting for the Great Day to arrive know that the Human Race is going to thrive. When we step out of the darkness and meditate on The Light, we gain insight about how we will become all that we were originally meant to be because that is our destiny.

It was foretold long ago that the breaking of the mould cast for our Civilisation was so that in the New Dawn there will be a greater level of realisation of our true orientation. Guided by Heavenly Beings in the way of Grace, all that is going to occur will establish us as a Race of Higher Evolved Beings, thereby bringing full circle the Atlantean Story; for The Almighty One has decreed that Atlantis is to be restored to its former glory. This is so that our long awaited, divinely timed, rebirth can be at the place that used to be called, Heaven on Earth.

---

[1] Selected Poems, Francis Thompson

www.ingramcontent.com/pod-product-compliance
Lightning Source LLC
Chambersburg PA
CBHW041927090426
42743CB00021B/3463